WHEN BEDS DON'T MOVE

How Flow Physics™ Reveals the Hidden Breakdowns Costing Hospitals Millions

By Donald Sipp Jr., MBA, RESE, CHESP, CHTI-2, CMIP, PMP

First published 2026

Any resemblance to specific organizations or people is coincidental.

ISBN: 979-8-9960313-0-6 (Paperback)

ISBN: 979-8-9960313-4-4 (Hardcover)

ISBN: 979-8-9960313-1-3 (eBook)

For permissions and inquiries:

Info@ImpactTrainingCompany.com

ImpactTrainingCompany.com

Printed in the United States of America

DEDICATION

For my mother, Cenia Ann Owens,

whose strength, courage, and love shaped the foundation of who I am.

Your journey inspires every page of this work.

And for my father, Donald Sipp, Sr.

who instilled in me the discipline to show up, the pride to do the work well,

and the belief that effort, repeated daily, builds everything that lasts.

For my children: Donald Aiden, Morgan Michael, Laila, and Dajan,

You are my purpose, my legacy, and my greatest motivation.

Everything I build is for you.

And for every EVS worker, transporter, linen technician, supervisor, and leader

who keeps hospitals moving, often without recognition.

This book is dedicated to you.

You are the heartbeat of patient flow.

Foreword

It is a privilege to write this foreword for Donald Sipp's book, When Beds Don't Move.

I first met Donald after contacting Georgie Shockey, co-owner of Ruck-Shockey & Associates, in search of expertise to help address challenges within our organization's Environmental Services department. From our very first conversation, I was impressed by Donald's depth of knowledge, practical experience, and thoughtful approach to improving healthcare operations.

Donald didn't simply offer recommendations. He provided a comprehensive assessment that met and exceeded my expectations. His knowledge and expertise helped guide our organization in the right direction, leading to significant improvements in patient throughput and a greater understanding of the critical role Environmental Services plays in the overall success of a healthcare system. The strategies and insights he shared enabled our team to improve operational efficiency, reduce delays, and create a more effective patient flow process that benefited both our patients and our caregivers.

Too often, Environmental Services is viewed as a support function rather than a strategic partner in patient care. Donald understands that every delayed discharge, every room waiting to be cleaned, and every bed sitting idle has a direct impact on patients, caregivers, and an organization's ability to deliver timely, high-quality care. His ability to connect operational efficiency with patient outcomes is what sets him apart.

This book provides a holistic approach to how support services can work together to improve patient flow and operational outcomes. Donald demonstrates that achieving efficient throughput is not the responsibility of a single department but a coordinated effort across Environmental Services, nursing, patient transport, bed management, and other essential support teams. By viewing these functions as interconnected parts of the patient care continuum, healthcare organizations can reduce delays, increase bed availability, enhance the patient experience, and improve overall organizational performance.

When Beds Don't Move captures the insight, experience, and leadership that Donald has demonstrated throughout his career. More than a discussion of Environmental Services, this book serves as a practical guide for healthcare leaders who are committed to improving patient flow, strengthening collaboration across departments, and achieving operational excellence. Whether you are an executive, clinician, or support services professional, you will find practical strategies that can be implemented to create lasting improvements in patient care and organizational performance.

I am grateful to Georgie Shockey for introducing me to Donald and even more grateful for the opportunity to benefit from his expertise. His guidance helped our organization achieve measurable and lasting improvements in patient throughput, and I am confident this book will help other healthcare organizations realize similar results.

I recommend "When Beds Don't Move" to you and encourage you to read it with an open mind. The insights contained in these pages have the potential to transform how you think about support services, patient flow, and the essential collaboration required to ensure that every patient receives timely, efficient, and compassionate care.

Antoinette "Toni" Watkins MS, RDN

System Director of Food, Nutrition & Environmental Services

Riverside Health System

Acknowledgments

I want to express my deepest gratitude to everyone who has shaped my life, my work, and the ideas within this book.

To my mother, Cenia Ann Owens, whose love, guidance, and strength laid the foundation for the man I became. Your journey continues to inspire me, and your memory lives in every lesson I share.

To my father, Donald Sipp Sr., thank you for your presence, your encouragement, and the values you instilled in me.

To my children: Donald Aiden, Morgan Michael, Laila, and Dajan, you are my motivation, my purpose, and the legacy I am building. Everything I strive for, I strive for you.

To my siblings: Victoria, Whitney, and William: thank you for your love, your support, and the strength we have always shared as a family.

To my extended family and friends, each of you has shaped a part of who I am. Even if I do not mention every name on this page, your presence has mattered, and I am grateful for you.

To the managers, supervisors, and leaders I have worked with and worked for over the years: thank you for trusting me, challenging me, and allowing me to lead alongside you. The lessons learned in those hallways, offices, command centers, EVS closets, transport bays, and conference rooms shaped the insights in this book.

To every EVS worker, transporter, linen technician, dispatcher, and supervisor I have had the privilege of working with, you are the warmth, the movement, and the heartbeat of the hospital. Your dedication, often unseen but always essential, is the true engine of patient flow. This book stands on your shoulders.

To my colleagues at Ruck-Shockey Associates, Inc., thank you for the collaboration, the partnership, and the shared commitment to improving healthcare operations. I am honored to be part of such a talented and mission-driven team.

To those who offered mentorship, perspective, and support, formally or informally: thank you for believing in me and challenging me to grow.

Finally, to anyone who has ever worked in a hospital and felt the pressure of movement, the strain of delays, or the weight of responsibility, this book is also for you. Your work matters, and your impact is far greater than you may ever realize.

TABLE OF CONTENTS

TABLE OF CONTENTS *(continued)*

PART THREE · **Holding the System**

PART ONE
The Framework

Understanding the invisible system that governs hospital movement.

Introduction: How Hospitals Lose the Day

Hospitals talk about capacity constantly. Dashboards measure it. Leadership meetings debate it. Strategic plans attempt to expand it.

Yet the crisis most hospitals face every day is not a shortage of beds.

It is a shortage of movement.

At 7:06 a.m. on a Tuesday, a 420-bed regional hospital had three beds physically available on a medical-surgical floor. The ED had two admitted patients waiting. Transport was staffed. Placement was at the desk.

By 8:30 a.m., the ED had five holds. The OR was flagging a PACU backup. Leadership was on a call asking why the morning had "gone sideways."

Nothing unusual had happened. No callouts. No surge. No equipment failure.

What had happened: the linen cart for the high-turnover corridor had been stocked out of sequence the night before. One EVS tech lost eleven minutes retrieving supplies for the first room. Transport's first cycle shifted. Two admits stacked instead of spacing. Nursing absorbed them simultaneously during a medication pass. Placement lost its matching rhythm.

By the time leadership noticed the pressure, the cause was ninety minutes old and three departments upstream.

The Sequence That Repeats Every Morning

6:47 a.m.

A linen cart is delivered to the wrong unit. The surgical floor gets Telemetry's linen. The surgical closet is short on high-use items.

7:04 a.m.

An EVS technician enters the first assigned room. The cabinet is missing towels. She walks back to the closet. Three minutes there. One minute searching. One minute back. Five minutes lost. The first room is not released on time.

7:09 a.m.

Transport's first cycle shifts. A patient in the ED who was ready to move is now waiting. The ED hold clock starts.

7:23 a.m.

Placement sequences two admits simultaneously because the first bed was expected to open by now. It hasn't. Both moves are stuck behind the same delayed room.

7:51 a.m.

Nursing on two floors absorbs back-to-back admissions during the morning medication pass. Both charge nurses are now managing three simultaneous tasks instead of one.

8:30 a.m.

The ED board shows four holds. The house supervisor called an escalation. The surgical schedule flags a potential PACU backup. Leadership asks: why is this morning so heavy?

8:47 a.m.

The linen cart is still on the wrong floor.

No one traces the 8:30 pressure back to 6:47. The escalation call discusses staffing. Communication. Volume. The actual cause, a misdelivered cart and a five-minute supply detour, never comes up. It will happen again tomorrow.

This sequence is not unusual. In most hospitals, some version of it happens every day.

What makes it a flow problem rather than a logistics problem is this: the people involved are not failing. The EVS tech did exactly what she was trained to do. The transporter responded the moment the room released. The nurses managed the admits professionally. The house supervisor called the escalation at the right time.

The system failed. Not the people. And because the system failure was invisible, untracked, and owned by no one, it will repeat with the same consequences tomorrow morning.

Here is the part that matters most: you have probably sat in that 8:30 escalation call. You have probably heard staffing cited. Volume cited. Communication cited. You may have left with action items about huddles, or escalation protocols, or staffing ratios. And the next morning, the pressure returned at the same time, for the same reasons, because nothing discussed in that call had anything to do with a linen cart delivered to the wrong unit at 6:47 a.m.

That is not a failure of leadership. It is a failure of visibility. The cause of your morning pressure is almost never where you are looking for it. It is upstream, it is small, it is structural, and it happened before most of your leaders arrived at work. The hospital is not reacting to the day. It is inheriting a sequence that was already broken.

Once you see that, you cannot unsee it. And once you name it, you can fix it.

That is what this book is about.

The same question gets asked every day in hospitals across the country: if beds are open, why can't patients move?

This is the Patient Flow Paradox. A hospital can have available beds and still function as if it is completely full. The reason is simple.

Capacity and movement are not the same thing.

A bed only matters when it activates at the moment a patient needs it. If activation is delayed by timing gaps, sequencing failures, or readiness problems, the hospital experiences gridlock even when beds exist on paper. Most hospitals try to solve this by focusing on people: adding staff, increasing communication, creating escalation meetings. These efforts rarely fix the underlying problem. Not because the people are incapable, but because the issue is structural.

The visible symptoms are chaos. The underlying cause is structure.

Patient flow follows patterns. Once those patterns are understood, delays become predictable and preventable. This book reveals the system behind hospital movement: the Flow Operating System™. Inside every hospital, invisible operational forces determine whether patients move smoothly or whether pressure builds. Throughout this book you will see how those forces interact, including:

- The Stagnation Gap™, where hospitals quietly lose the momentum needed to start the day
- The laws of Flow Physics™, which explain how timing, sequencing, velocity, and load shape hospital movement
- Activation Windows™, which determine whether departments enter the day aligned or already behind
- The Support Services Chain™, the operational engine that converts clinical decisions into real bed movement
- The governance discipline required to keep the system aligned

I have spent more than two decades inside hospitals studying these patterns. Not from the outside, not in theory, but in the corridors, the EVS closets, the transport bays, and the command centers where operational pressure actually lives. Academic medical centers, regional health systems, community hospitals. Different cities, different leadership, different staffing. The same collapse, repeating.

Once that system becomes visible, flow stops feeling mysterious. Delays become measurable. Capacity, often assumed to be permanently constrained, can begin to unlock.

A note on sources and methodology: the operational patterns and case scenarios in this book reflect direct field observation across more than two decades of hospital assessments spanning academic medical centers, regional health systems, and community hospitals. Composite case scenarios are illustrative representations of recurring patterns and do not represent any single institution or individual. The financial consequences of the flow failures described throughout this book are supported by published research. Studies published in the Annals of Emergency Medicine and peer-reviewed healthcare operations literature document that ED boarding alone costs hospitals millions of dollars annually in extended care costs, lost throughput, and suppressed capacity. The Flow Physics™ framework presented here is not a theoretical model. It is a pattern that already exists in your hospital. This book makes it visible.

The First Failure of the Day

Hospitals don't begin the day in readiness. They begin the day in Drift™.

You feel this the moment you walk onto any unit. The hospital is already behind, and the first move of the day hasn't even happened yet. Discharges aren't ready. Orders are pending. Rooms aren't cleared. EVS doesn't have a clean first target. Transport has nowhere to send the first patient. Before the sun rises, the first sequence of the day is already broken.

The collapse doesn't happen at noon, or during the surge, or when the ED starts boarding. It happens the moment the hospital enters the day without alignment. Nights are built to stabilize, not to move. Day shift isn't creating Drift. They're inheriting it.

The chain is mechanical:

- If the first discharge is late, EVS starts late.
- If EVS starts late, Transport starts late.
- If Transport starts late, Placement starts late.
- If Placement starts late, the ED boards earlier.
- If the ED boards earlier, the hospital loses capacity by mid-morning.

Every department believes it is responding to the problem. In reality, it is responding to the effect of an earlier Drift. By mid-morning, leaders ask the same questions they ask every day: Why is the ED backing up? Why aren't beds moving? Who's not communicating?

These questions assume the collapse is caused by people. The collapse is caused by timing.

Hospitals measure everything except the one thing that decides the whole day:

First Movement Time™ (FMT™).

FMT™ is the timestamp of the first confirmed patient move of the day. It drives flow, pressure, Drift, and capacity recovery. Yet almost no hospital measures it, monitors it, or manages it.

What FMT Measurement Reveals: A Composite Case

> *In a 350-bed regional medical center, leaders consistently reported that the ED "got busy early." Morning escalation calls started at 9:00 a.m. Staffing and communication were the recurring explanations.*
>
> *When the hospital began tracking First Movement Time™, a different picture emerged. The average FMT was 7:34 a.m., but on high-*

pressure days it slipped to 8:11 a.m. Every day FMT exceeded 7:45 a.m., ED holds by mid-morning increased by an average of 40 percent. There had been no staffing change. No communication failure. The only variable was when the first movement happened.

Once the hospital set a protected FMT target of 7:20 a.m. and assigned ownership to a single operational coordinator, the pattern broke. Over ninety days, mid-morning ED holds declined measurably and morning escalation calls dropped by more than half.

Composite scenario representing patterns observed across multiple hospital assessments.

The Stagnation Gap™

Even when timing slips are not catastrophic, hospitals lose the day in another way: the Stagnation Gap™.

This is the invisible period between "the day has started" and "the hospital is actually moving." Every hospital has one. Staff are working. Tasks are completing. Documentation is updating. But beds aren't moving.

Everyone looks busy. The hospital is stuck.

The Gap looks like momentum. It is the system stalling while people inside it work harder than ever. The morning isn't a preparation window. It is the only time the hospital can get ahead. If that window stagnates, the rest of the day collapses with predictable force.

In a slackless system, the distinctions that matter are not about effort:

- Work is not movement.
- Movement is not readiness.
- Readiness is not timing.
- Timing is not sequencing.
- Sequencing is not flow.

Most organizations never see these distinctions. They see effort and miss alignment. They see activity and miss architecture, because timing is invisible, not measured, and owned by no one; the Stagnation Gap becomes permanent.

Over time, it shapes culture. It convinces the organization that early stagnation is normal, that late discharges are expected, that the ED should live in pressure. Once a hospital normalizes the Gap, it stops seeing delay as delay. It sees delay as routine. This is how Drift becomes identity.

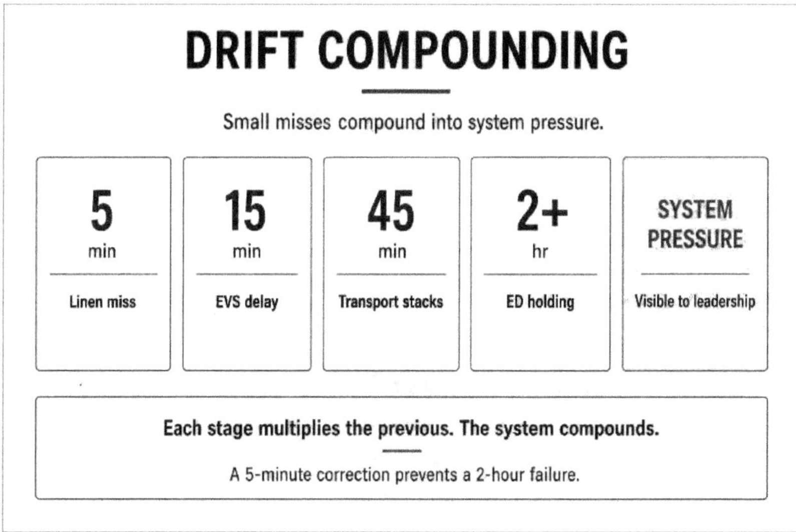

Figure 1: Drift Compounding

Measuring the Gap: A Composite Case

At a 500-bed academic medical center, nursing directors reported that mornings felt "busy but unproductive." Staff were active by 6:30 a.m. Yet the first confirmed bed move rarely occurred before 8:45 a.m.

When operations leaders began auditing activity versus movement, the Stagnation Gap became visible. On average, 2 hours and 15 minutes elapsed between shift start and first movement. During that window, more than 40 tasks were completed across units, none of which directly enabled a patient move.

Once leaders named the Gap and restructured morning sequencing around movement triggers rather than activity milestones, the Gap compressed to under 45 minutes within sixty days. Downstream ED boarding pressure dropped consistently in the weeks that followed.

Composite scenario representing patterns observed across multiple hospital assessments.

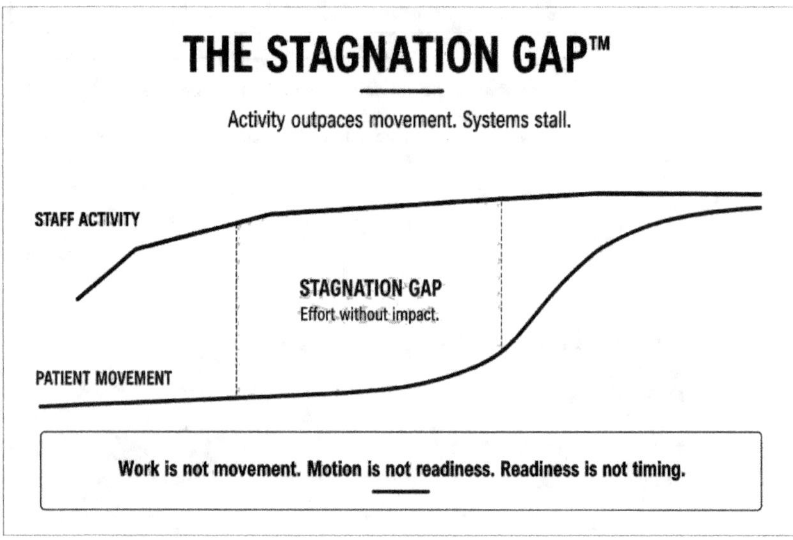

Figure 2: The Stagnation Gap

What This Book Does

The Stagnation Gap is not a slow morning. It is structural delay wearing the uniform of normal operations. Hospitals lose the day not in the surge but in the quiet stretch before it, when activity is high, movement is absent, and no alarm has fired.

Naming it is the first act of leadership. You cannot close a gap you have not seen.

The Flow Operating System™ is not a new program. It is a description of forces already operating in your hospital every day. The question is whether those forces are aligned, or quietly compounding against you. Flow Physics™ explains why. The seven engines in Part Two show where those laws are honored or broken. The governance chapters that follow show what it takes to hold them.

Hospitals do not struggle because beds are full. They struggle because the system that unlocks those beds is invisible.

This book makes that system visible.

Movement inside a hospital is not luck. It is architecture. And architecture can be fixed.

CHAPTER 1

Flow Physics™

How the Invisible System Creates the Visible Day

Every hospital experiences the same recurring pressure points: delays, bottlenecks, crowded EDs, slow discharges, backed-up ORs, late nights, and constant escalation. Leaders can describe the symptoms. Teams work hard to fight them. Yet few can explain why the same patterns unfold day after day.

Flow Physics™ describes the operating rules beneath the visible hospital. It explains how the day accelerates, how engines fall out of rhythm, and why small early slips can grow into system-wide pressure by mid-morning.

The visible hospital shows the tasks.

The invisible hospital shows the mechanics.

People can be motivated, skilled, collaborative, and fully staffed, and the hospital can still break. Flow is shaped by design, not effort.

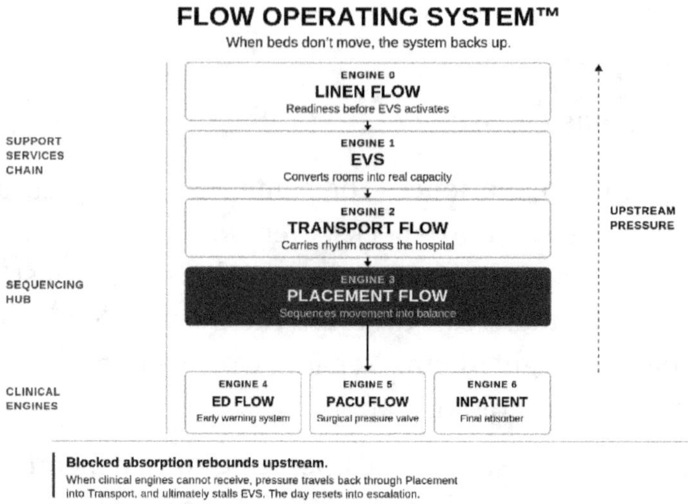

Figure 3: The Flow Operating System

Flow Physics™ explains what the hospital looks like when its engines are aligned, and why it collapses when they are not.

The Five Laws of Flow Physics™

Across hospitals of every size and structure, the same operational patterns repeat. These five laws describe the forces leaders experience every day but rarely see clearly.

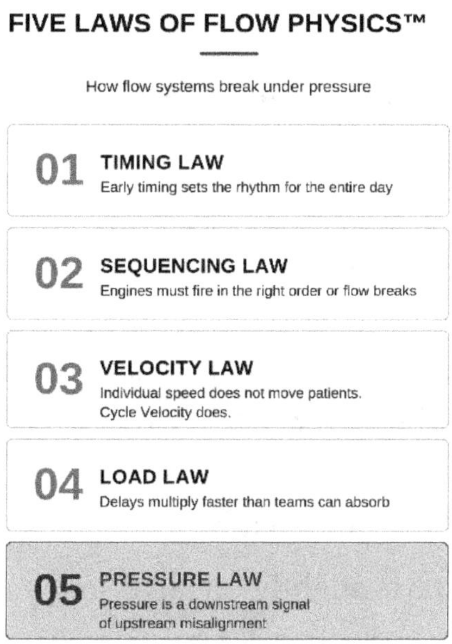

Figure 4: The Five Laws of Flow Physics

- The Timing Law: early timing sets the rhythm for the entire day.
- The Sequencing Law: engines must fire in the right order, or flow breaks.
- The Velocity Law: individual speed doesn't move patients. Cycle Velocity™ does.
- The Load Law: delays multiply faster than teams can absorb.
- The Pressure Law: pressure is a downstream signal of upstream misalignment.

Once you understand these laws, the daily chaos starts to make sense.

What feels random becomes predictable. What feels personal becomes structural. What looks like a performance problem often turns out to be physics.

1. The Timing Law

Flow depends on when engines activate, not how hard people work.

Most hospitals win or lose the day in the first hour. A small timing slip at the start quietly shapes everything that follows.

Even a brief delay propagates through the system:

- EVS starts slightly off rhythm.
- Transport's first cycles shift.
- Nursing receives early admissions later than expected.
- Placement can't match beds at the right time.
- ED holds grow.
- The OR loses predictability.

When timing slips, effort rises. When timing holds, effort drops.

A hospital that hits its early timing feels lighter for the rest of the day.

A hospital that misses it spends the day trying to recover.

2. The Sequencing Law

Engines must fire in the right order or the system fractures.

Every hospital has a natural operational sequence.

Linen → EVS → Transport → Nursing → Placement → ED → OR

When the sequence holds, flow is predictable. When it breaks, delays spread to departments that didn't create them.

Signs of sequence failure:

- EVS waiting for linen.
- Transport waiting for EVS.
- Nursing waiting for Transport.
- Placement waiting for Nursing.
- The ED holding because upstream movement stalled.
- OR cases stacking because beds weren't available.

Only early alignment preserves sequence.

3. The Velocity Law

People moving fast is not the same as the hospital moving fast.

Cycle Velocity™, not individual speed, determines how patients move.

Cycle Velocity™ is the time it takes an engine to complete a full operational cycle. A hospital can be full of hardworking people and still move slowly if its engines aren't cycling at the pace the system requires.

Cycle Velocity™ drops when:

- early timing drifts
- assignments bunch
- handoffs are uneven
- readiness varies between units
- early cycles start late
- tasks are batched instead of sequenced

Effort can't restore lost velocity. Only alignment can.

4. The Load Law

Delays multiply faster than teams can absorb.

A small delay upstream frequently becomes a much larger delay downstream:

- stacked Transport cycles
- Nursing workload spikes
- Placement losing matching rhythm
- ED filling earlier
- OR losing predictability
- discharges sliding later

Load grows faster than people can clear it.

Once load expands beyond capacity, the hospital shifts from moving patients to managing backlog.

5. The Pressure Law

Pressure is a downstream signal of upstream misalignment.

Pressure appears downstream after:

- timing drifts
- sequence fractures
- velocity drops
- load multiplies
- Activation Windows™ are missed

Teams under pressure often feel blamed for problems they didn't create. They are simply the first place upstream physics becomes visible.

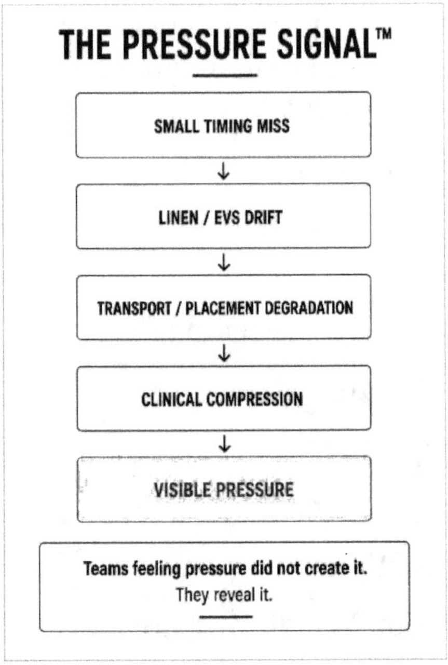

Figure 5: The Pressure Signal

Activation Windows™, Where the Day Is Won or Lost

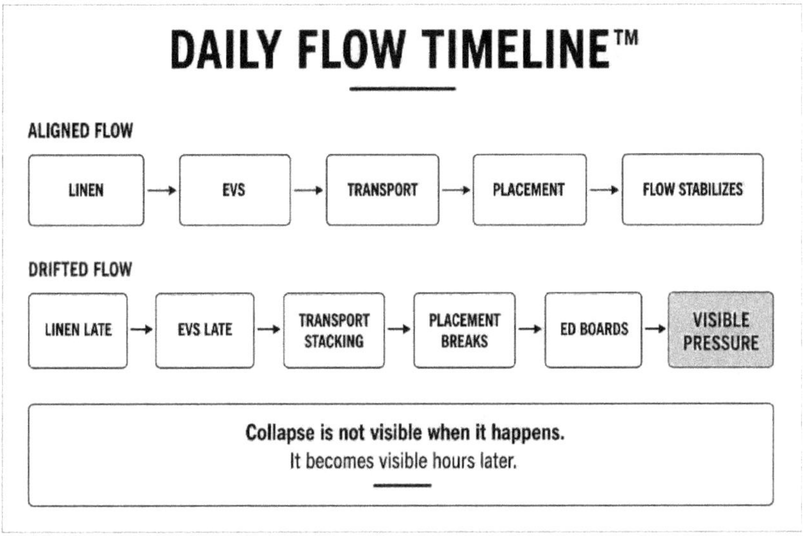

Figure 6: Daily Flow Timeline

An Activation Window™ is a narrow period when an engine must activate to keep the system aligned. These windows are small, quiet, and unforgiving.

Examples:

- EVS entering the first room on time
- Transport beginning its first cycle in sync with EVS
- Nursing receiving early admits at the expected pace
- Placement matching beds as soon as they open
- ED decompressing during its early flow period
- OR receiving predictable postoperative beds

When Activation Windows™ are hit, the day flows. When they are missed, the day drifts.

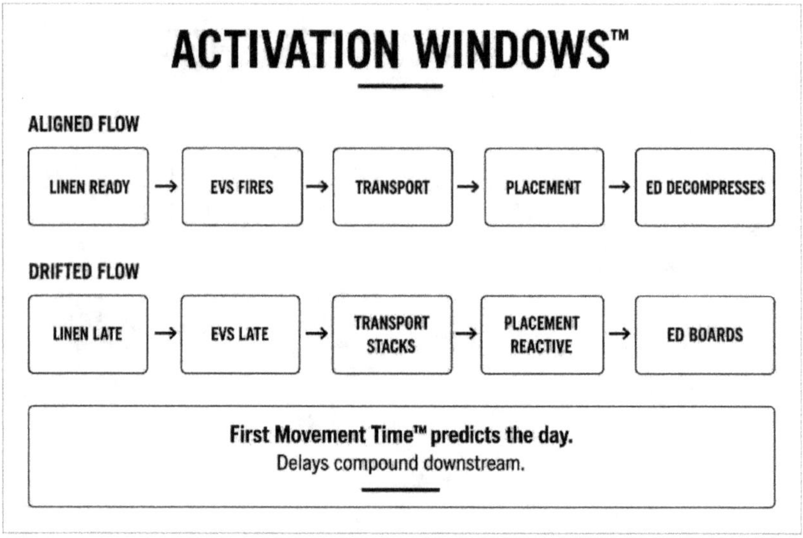

Figure 7: Activation Windows

Why Activation Window Misses Go Unnoticed

Activation Window misses leave no footprint:

- no alarms
- no dashboard alerts
- no escalation

Hours later:

- The ED fills.
- The OR stalls.
- Discharges slide.
- Nursing overloads.
- Transport is overwhelmed.
- EVS receives a wave of calls.

What feels sudden is simply the moment upstream drift becomes visible.

Cycle Loss™, How the System Quietly Slows Down

Cycle Loss™ occurs when the time between cycles increases even though tasks are still being completed. It is subtle, and it accumulates.

Cycle Loss™ grows from:

- minor timing drift
- uneven handoffs
- short waits between steps
- readiness gaps
- slight mis-sequencing

Cycle after cycle, the system slows until the gap becomes too large to hide. As Cycle Loss accumulates, Cycle Velocity™ drops. The engine completes fewer cycles per hour, and downstream engines wait longer between each one.

How Cycle Loss™ Multiplies

A few minutes lost upstream can become:

- a shifted Transport cycle
- slower Nursing receive times
- delayed matching
- earlier ED boarding

- OR pressure by midday

Each engine amplifies the drift of the engine before it.

Engine Misalignment™, When Engines Fall Out of Rhythm

Engine Misalignment™ often appears as:

- EVS "behind"
- Transport "slow"
- Nursing "overloaded"
- Placement "unresponsive"
- ED "backed up"
- OR "delayed"

These aren't failures. They are symptoms of early misalignment.

Why Perfect Teamwork Still Fails

Some of the hardest days happen in hospitals where teams are communicating well, responding quickly, and working hard.

But if early engines were already out of rhythm, even slightly, the entire hospital inherits that drift.

Perfect teamwork cannot overcome misaligned physics.

Alignment creates flow; teamwork amplifies alignment.

Why Leaders Must Think in Physics, Not Personalities

Behavior shows the symptoms. Physics shows the cause.

When leaders shift to physics-based thinking:

- friction drops
- communication quiets
- ED decompresses earlier
- OR becomes predictable
- discharges stabilize
- burnout decreases
- pressure disappears

Not because people suddenly changed, but because the system began supporting them.

The first place these laws are honored or broken is Engine 0, Linen Flow™. The chapter that follows shows why the day begins before EVS touches the first room, and how a stocking sequence set the night before can decide whether the hospital enters the morning aligned or already drifting.

Flow Physics in Practice: A Composite Case

> *At a 340-bed regional hospital, an operations director had spent three years working with department heads to improve throughput. Each initiative produced temporary improvement. Within weeks, pressure returned. The pattern was consistent enough that leadership had quietly stopped believing the gains were real.*

When an operational review introduced the Flow Physics™ framework, the director began mapping what she had previously seen as isolated problems onto the five laws. The Timing Law explained why Monday pressure always peaked by 9:00 a.m., regardless of weekend volume. The Sequencing Law explained why Transport chronically stacked requests despite being adequately staffed. The Load Law explained why a single delayed discharge at 7:30 a.m. reliably produced ED holding by 10:00 a.m.

The framework did not add new work. It changed the questions. Instead of asking which department was behind, leadership began asking which law had been violated and at what time. Within thirty days, the operations director had identified three recurring Activation Window misses that collectively explained more than 60 percent of the hospital's chronic morning pressure.

The fixes were small. The stocking sequence in two linen closets was corrected. EVS room assignments were reordered by placement priority. A single Transport coordinator began watching for request clustering at 7:15

a.m. rather than waiting for the board to fill. The gains held, because the correction addressed physics rather than symptoms.

> *Composite scenario representing patterns observed across multiple hospital assessments.*

Flow Physics™ does not describe how hospitals should work.

It describes how they actually work.

The five laws are not aspirational; they are operational.

The engines in Part Two are where these laws are either honored or broken. Engine 0 is where the day begins.

PART TWO
The Seven Engines

Where Flow Physics™ is honored or broken.

CHAPTER 2

Engine 0: Linen Flow™

The Engine Before the Engines

The most expensive mistakes in a hospital often happen before 7:00 a.m., in spaces almost no one is watching. By the time leaders feel the pressure, the damage is already done.

Most hospitals assume the day begins when EVS steps into the first room. That is when the day becomes visible, not when it actually begins.

Flow starts before sunrise, before dashboards refresh, and before any request hits Transport. It starts in the quiet, overlooked spaces where Linen Flow™ sets the conditions for whether the hospital enters the day aligned or drifting.

Linen is not just a supply function. Linen is the hospital's first timing constraint. When Engine 0 is aligned, downstream engines begin the day in rhythm. When Engine 0 drifts, the hospital can start behind before anyone realizes it.

Hospitals feel pressure by mid-morning. The root cause often appears much earlier, in a closet, a cart, or a stocking sequence that slipped before the first shift arrived.

Engine 0 sets the readiness, timing, and early Cycle Velocity™ that shape the entire day.

The First Activation Window™

Every operational engine depends on an Activation Window™, a narrow time slice when that engine must activate to preserve flow. These windows rarely announce themselves, but they reliably indicate whether the hospital is aligned.

Linen controls the first window.

When the morning par is accurate, stocked in sequence, delivered on time, and ready before EVS activates, the early morning unfolds with stability:

- EVS enters the first room without delay.
- Transport begins its first cycle on time.
- Nursing receives admissions earlier.
- Placement matches sooner.
- The ED decompresses.
- The OR maintains predictable early flow.

The hospital's first hour depends on a function most leaders rarely round on or measure in operational terms. This is not preference; it is physics: timing drives sequence, sequence drives velocity, and velocity determines load.

When Linen Flow™ slips, every downstream engine begins the day compensating.

The First Room Rule™ in Action

At 7:04 a.m., an EVS tech walks into the first assigned room of the day. The cabinet is missing a single towel bundle.

The tech turns around and walks back to the closet.

Three minutes to walk there. One minute to search. One minute to return.

Five minutes are lost, before the first room is even released.

Those five minutes often translate into:

- EVS misses its Activation Window™.
- Transport's first call shifts.
- The first admission stalls.
- Nursing absorbs early delay.
- Placement loses sequence.
- The ED holds patients longer.
- The OR receives beds later than expected.

Downstream engines feel the impact. Upstream causes stay invisible.

This is the First Room Rule™:

The engine that controls the first room shapes the entire day. Linen controls that room long before anyone else does.

Why Linen Is Underestimated

Many hospitals assume linen is simple, inexpensive, and predictable. In reality, Linen Flow™ is variable, complex, and tied tightly to turnover, acuity, and demand patterns.

Linen is a readiness engine. It is the foundation every downstream engine stands on.

When Engine 0 is aligned, the hospital can start in rhythm. When Engine 0 drifts, early timing fractures and drift spreads downstream. Readiness breaks upstream long before pressure appears downstream.

The Readiness Engine

Readiness can be validated. It is visible in sequence, timing, and structure, not emotion or assumption.

A unit is operationally ready only when Linen has:

- Correct par levels.
- Correct stocking sequence.
- Correct stocking timing.
- Accurate placement of high-use items.
- Replenishment matched to unit-level patterns.
- Alignment to the unit's demand curve.
- Verification before EVS activates.

If any of these fail, EVS begins behind. Transport inherits delay. Nursing inherits backlog. Placement loses rhythm. ED pressure rises, and the OR loses early stability.

Upstream readiness failures do more damage than downstream performance issues.

Par Is Not Inventory, Par Is Timing

Hospitals often treat par as a number. Par is a timing condition, not an inventory metric.

Incorrect par breaks the Activation Window, not just convenience.

When par is off:

- EVS loses minutes backtracking for supplies.
- Those minutes break readiness.
- Broken readiness becomes sequence drift.
- Sequence drift lowers Cycle Velocity™.
- Velocity loss magnifies load faster than teams can absorb.

A closet can appear full and still fail its timing requirement. A closet can be partially filled yet fully support flow.

Timing outweighs volume every time.

The Transport–Linen Lag Effect™

When Linen Flow™ slips, Transport inherits the delay even when Transport performs well.

Transport arrives to rooms that are not ready. Cycles shift. Velocity slows. Early admits arrive late. Nursing absorbs the delay. Placement loses its matching rhythm. ED holds longer. OR decompresses later.

This is the Transport–Linen Lag Effect™:

Linen-driven drift produces wasted Transport cycles, and wasted cycles slow the entire hospital.

Transport often takes the blame. Transport rarely causes the problem.

The Linen Geography Problem™

Closet placement and layout heavily influence early-morning velocity. Geography is rarely engineered intentionally, yet it changes the Activation Window more than almost any other factor.

Common geography failures include:

- closets too far from high-turnover rooms
- closets sized for outdated patterns
- multiple units sharing a single closet
- shelving arranged against workflow
- closets placed for convenience instead of demand
- distance-induced detours that add unnecessary travel time

Distance creates drift. Every unnecessary step erodes timing.

A closet located even 50 steps farther from priority rooms can add meaningful travel time per tech per shift, enough to break the Activation Window™ even when everything else is correct.

Geography can anchor flow or guarantee drift.

For the Yellow and Red signals that mark where Linen Flow™ is approaching, or already breaking, the Activation Window, see the Yellow vs. Red Signal Matrix introduced in Chapter 3.

Stocking Sequence, Flow Engineering, Not Shelf Filling

In many hospitals, stocking is treated as "fill the closet."

But stocking is not a supply task; it is flow engineering.

Stocking determines:

- Which rooms EVS can start.
- Which rooms EVS must delay.
- How EVS moves across geography.
- When Transport begins its first cycle.
- When admissions can arrive.
- How Placement matches.
- When the ED decompresses.
- When PACU releases.
- When the OR receives beds.

Stocking for convenience creates drift. Stocking for sequence creates flow.

A single out-of-sequence cart delivered at 6:45 a.m. can disrupt more of the hospital than many leaders realize.

Sequence is operational physics, not preference.

The Cart That Shifted the Morning

At 6:47 a.m., a linen cart meant for a surgical unit is mistakenly delivered to Telemetry.

The Telemetry closet ends up overfilled with low-priority items.

The surgical closet receives its linen late.

EVS begins out of sequence. Transport arrives to rooms not ready. Nursing receives early admits behind schedule. The ED holds patients longer. PACU fills earlier than expected. OR cases feel the shift before mid-morning.

The cart did not look like a crisis.

But it changed the order of the morning, and order is everything.

Linen Flow Demand Variance™

Every unit has a distinct Linen Flow Demand Curve. Stocking every unit the same guarantees mismatch and drift.

- ICU, steady, low variance, high urgency
- Med/Surg, high turnover, unpredictable bursts
- Surgical floors, demand tied to OR case blocks
- Telemetry, steady, moderate turnover
- ED, high volatility
- Labor and Delivery, rapid swings
- Behavioral Health, slow and predictable

Demand is never flat. Demand is curved.

When Linen Flow™ does not follow each unit's curve, drift begins early and spreads quickly.

Drift always spreads.

The Seven-Day Linen Rhythm

Most hospitals think in one-day rhythms. Linen Flow™ operates in seven-day cycles.

Weekend Drift™ is one of the most consistent patterns observed across the industry.

Common drivers include:

- reduced linen staffing
- delayed weekend deliveries
- higher turnover from family visits
- inconsistent mid-cycle replenishment
- closets stocked for volume instead of velocity
- missing a verification layer

By early Monday, the system can already be misaligned:

- Linen may be off par.
- EVS may begin behind.
- Transport may inherit shifted cycles.
- Nursing may receive admits late.
- Placement may lose matching rhythm.
- ED may feel early pressure.
- OR may struggle to decompress.

Monday often inherits drift created on Sunday.

The Sunday Drift That Broke Monday

At 7:03 a.m. Monday, Transport is already stacked.

The ED board shows early pressure. Nursing is juggling admits. Placement is escalating.

It feels like a heavy-volume morning.

But Monday is not the cause. Sunday is.

Sunday patterns included:

- reduced linen staffing
- delayed vendor delivery
- no mid-cycle replenishment
- closets stocked for convenience
- surgical units stocked last
- no verification layer

By Monday morning:

- EVS was behind.
- Transport cycles had shifted.
- Nursing received admits late.
- Placement lost early matching.
- ED held patients.
- OR lost early decompression.

Monday only inherited the drift.

The Linen Flow Cycle™

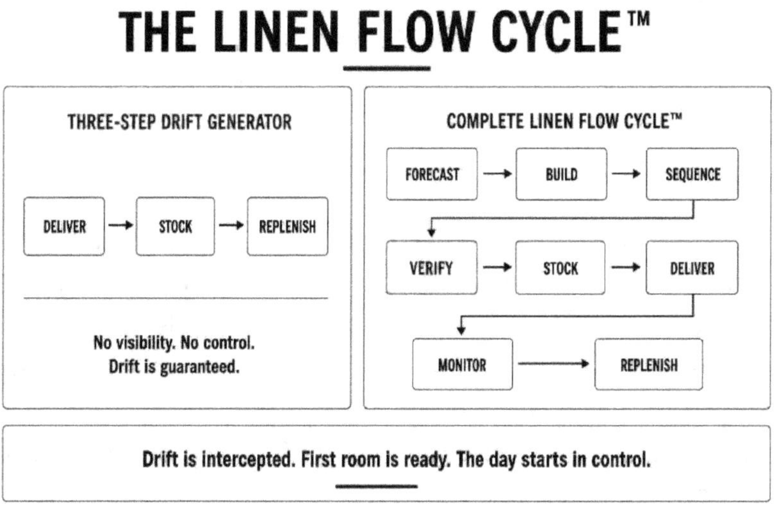

Figure 8: The Linen Flow Cycle

Most hospitals treat Linen Flow™ as:

Deliver → Stock → Replenish

This is not a cycle. It is a drift generator.

The complete Linen Flow Cycle™ includes:

- Forecast
- Build
- Sequence
- Deliver
- Stock
- Verify
- Monitor
- Replenish

Eight steps support alignment. Three steps support drift.

The five steps most hospitals skip are not minor details. Each one carries a specific failure mode that surfaces hours later, in a different department, with no obvious tie back to its origin.

Forecast

Forecast estimates demand against the actual unit-level curve. ICU steady. Med/Surg variable. Surgical floors tied to OR blocks. Without a forecast, par levels are uniform across units that consume linen at very different rates. Surgical units run short by mid-morning. EVS detours to retrieve supplies. The Activation Window breaks before anyone notices it.

Build

Build assembles each cart against the demand pattern of the unit it is going to. Without Build, carts are loaded uniformly. High-use items end up in the wrong cart for the wrong unit. By 7:00 a.m., one closet is overstocked and another is short the items the first room needs.

Sequence

Sequence determines the order of stocking inside the closet, not just the order of delivery. Without Sequence, high-use items end up at the back of the shelf and low-priority items end up in front. The first EVS tech of the day reaches for a towel bundle and finds linen for a different unit on top of it. Five minutes are lost before the first room is released.

Verify

Verify is a single check before EVS activates that confirms the closet matches the morning demand. Without Verify, the assumption that the closet is ready replaces the fact of it. The first failure of the day is not detected until EVS is already inside the room.

Monitor

Monitor watches mid-cycle replenishment against actual consumption. Without Monitor, mid-day shortages appear without warning. Transport cycles shift in the early afternoon, Placement loses its matching rhythm, and the ED begins boarding for reasons no dashboard explains.

When these five steps are absent, the abbreviated three-step cycle (Deliver, Stock, Replenish) still completes. The closet still gets filled. The day still starts. But the system has lost every mechanism it had to detect drift before EVS inherits it. The Linen Flow Cycle™ is not eight steps because eight is thorough. It is eight steps because that is how many points of detection are required to keep the first engine from quietly failing.

The Financial Model, Engine 0™'s Hidden ROI

Hospitals often measure linen by product cost. The true cost shows up downstream:

- EVS overtime
- Transport overtime
- Nursing overtime
    - Contract labor
    - Extended length of stay
- ED boarding
- OR case delays
- PACU congestion
    - Late discharges
    - Placement stalls
    - Leadership escalation cycles
    - Burnout and turnover

Engine 0 influences every engine that follows. When Linen Flow™ aligns, the hospital experiences less friction, fewer escalations, and a smoother early rhythm. When Linen Flow™ drifts, every engine absorbs pressure it did not create.

Alignment compounds positively. Drift compounds negatively.

A single corrected Activation Window can stabilize:

- EVS's first rooms

- Transport's cycles
- early admission flow
- Nursing capacity
- Placement rhythm
- ED decompression
- OR predictability
- discharge momentum

Engine 0 is not peripheral. It is leverage.

The Closing Truth

Linen Drift does not only disrupt operations. It disrupts people. When Engine 0 slips, EVS feels blamed for delays it did not create. Transport feels behind before the day begins. Nurses feel overloaded early. Placement feels stuck. Leaders feel reactive.

Alignment changes that. Communication softens. Escalations drop. Handoffs improve. Teams feel supported rather than overwhelmed.

Fairness builds trust. Trust builds stability. Stability supports performance.

Engine 0 shapes how the hospital feels before it shapes how the hospital performs. Flow rarely begins in the first room; it begins with Linen Flow™. When the first engine is aligned, downstream engines start the day with stability. When it drifts, the hospital begins compensating before sunrise.

Engine 0 is leverage. The engines that follow depend on it.

Engine 0 in Practice: A Composite Case

At a 280-bed community hospital, leaders attributed chronic Monday-morning pressure to weekend volume. Escalation calls were routine by 8:30 a.m. EVS was consistently described as "running behind."

A Linen Flow™ assessment revealed that weekend stocking covered only 68 percent of the Monday demand curve for surgical and telemetry units. High-use items were positioned in back-of-closet locations. No verification step existed before EVS activation.

After restructuring weekend stocking protocols, repositioning high-use linen to front-of-closet placement, and introducing a 6:45 a.m. closet verification check, EVS's average first-room activation time moved from 7:28 a.m. to 7:09 a.m. Monday morning escalation calls declined. Transport and placement coordinators both reported noticeably smoother early sequencing. The sequence adjustment was positional: linen placement and stocking order were redesigned to match the Activation Window™, not just par levels.

Composite scenario representing patterns observed across multiple hospital assessments.

EVS and the First Room Rule

The next engine is EVS, the first visible engine, and the engine most often judged for delays that originate upstream.

But before Engine 1 can succeed, it must receive something from Engine 0: a ready first room.

The First Room Rule™ is the hinge point where invisible drift becomes visible delay. Everything that happens in Engine 0 is largely invisible to the rest of the hospital: no dashboard measures it, few escalation calls name it, and most leaders do not round on linen readiness at 6:45 a.m. But the moment EVS enters the first room, the invisible becomes visible. If the closet is ready, the sequence is correct, and the timing holds, EVS moves with momentum, and the morning stabilizes. If Engine 0 slips, EVS hesitates, detours, or compensates, and the hospital begins inheriting drift it cannot yet explain.

When Engine 0 delivers a ready first room at the right time, EVS enters that room with momentum. The morning begins with alignment. The Activation Window holds.

When Engine 0 delivers a late first room, a mis-stocked closet, or a wrong-sequence cart, EVS enters that room already compensating. The team is not behind because they are slow. They are behind because the first engine did not give them what they needed.

This is the most important transition in the hospital's operational day. Not a transition between departments. A transition between conditions.

Next: The Hidden Discipline

Engine 0 sets the condition. The Hidden Discipline chapter that follows explains the three forces that determine whether every engine enters the day aligned or already drifting: signals, timing, and readiness.

CHAPTER 3

The Hidden Discipline

Signals, Timing, and Readiness

This chapter is not itself an engine chapter. It establishes three cross-cutting disciplines that determine whether every engine in Part Two operates in alignment or in drift: signals, timing, and readiness. The Yellow vs. Red Signal Matrix that closes this chapter applies to all seven engines. Each engine chapter that follows assumes familiarity with the framework developed here.

Hospitals talk about staffing, beds, and capacity.

They rarely talk about signals, timing, and readiness, the three forces that determine whether downstream engines start the day aligned or already drifting.

Signals are how a hospital communicates. Timing is how a hospital stays in rhythm. Readiness is how a hospital converts intent into movement.

These are not clinical concepts. They are operational disciplines.

When they drift, every engine inherits the consequences.

Signals: The First Language of Flow

Hospitals move on signals: bed ready, patient ready, room released, placement confirmed, transport assigned.

When signals fire late or inconsistently:

- Engines pause.
- Decisions slow.
- Sequencing becomes uncertain.
- Movement hesitates.
- Drift begins.

Most delays begin with a simple truth:

The signal didn't fire when it should have.

Timing: The Protector of Flow

Even small timing misses multiply downstream.

If signals are the language, timing is the rhythm.

Hospitals collapse not because a single task was late, but because timing across multiple engines slipped in small increments.

- A room is returned seven minutes late.
- Placement sequences three minutes late.
- Transport pauses for verification.
- Nursing delays acceptance by four minutes.

These don't feel like failures.

But together, they break the morning.

Flow Physics™ is unforgiving:

Time lost early becomes pressure later.

Readiness: The Switch That Activates Movement

Readiness is not about effort. It is about alignment.

A patient can be clinically ready but operationally blocked. A bed can be clean but not released. A transport request can be triggered but not sequenced. A nurse can be available but not signaled.

Readiness means:

- Environment.
- Timing.
- Communication.
- The next engine.

Readiness exists only when all of these align at the same moment.

Without readiness, nothing moves, even when the staff is working hard.

What Drift Looks Like in Real Life

When signals, timing, and readiness drift, even slightly, the result is rarely dramatic. It looks like this:

At 7:46 a.m., a unit missed its readiness signal by nine minutes.

Transport paused, waiting for confirmation the room was truly ready.

EVS had completed the room, but the signal didn't release on time.

Placement held the admit because sequencing wasn't verified.

The ED kept the patient because the downstream engines were uncertain.

Nothing dramatic happened. No one made a major mistake.

But nine minutes of drift multiplied across the next three hours.

This is timing drift: invisible, quiet, and expensive.

When Signals, Timing, and Readiness Misalign

Drift is not binary. Systems do not move cleanly from "working" to "failed." They slide.

Leaders wait too long because red feels actionable. Red justifies urgency, escalation, and intervention. Yellow does not. Yellow feels ambiguous, debatable, and easy to tolerate.

But by the time a system turns red, the outcome is already determined. The real failure occurs earlier, at the moment green turns to yellow, when timing first slips, signals weaken, and readiness is assumed instead of verified. At that point, the system is already lost. It just hasn't announced it yet.

Reading the Signal: Yellow vs. Red by Engine

YELLOW vs. RED SIGNAL MATRIX™

YELLOW · DRIFT FORMING	
E0 LINEN	Sequence drift. EVS slowing.
E1 EVS	Priority misalignment.
E2 TRANSPORT	Queue instability.
E3 PLACEMENT	Load imbalance.
E4 ED	Waiting increasing.
E5 PACU	Wave overlap.
E6 INPATIENT	Discharge delay.

RED · OUTCOME LOCKED	
E0 LINEN	Par failure.
E1 EVS	First room missed.
E2 TRANSPORT	Stacking.
E3 PLACEMENT	Hold triggered.
E4 ED	Boarding surge.
E5 PACU	Capacity reached.
E6 INPATIENT	System rebound.

YELLOW is where you fix it. | RED is where you manage it.

Figure 9: Yellow vs. Red Signal Matrix

Leaders who understand the green-to-yellow-to-red slide can intervene before outcomes are determined. Yellow is not a minor inconvenience. Yellow is the system telling you what is about to happen. The following signals define what Yellow and Red look like for each engine.

Engine 0: Linen Flow

Yellow: Par levels are within range, but high-use items are positioned incorrectly in closets. Stocking is completed on time, but sequence is wrong. The verification step is skipped because the shift is moving fast. EVS begins without stopping, but the first room takes longer than expected.

Red: Par is visibly short on high-use items before EVS activates. Closets are stocked for the wrong unit demand curve. No verification has occurred. EVS enters the first room and immediately detours for supplies. The Activation Window is missed before 7:15 a.m.

Engine 1: EVS

Yellow: First room entry is on time, but the room sequence does not match placement priority. One isolation room is taking longer than planned and absorbing a tech. Rooms are being released in geographic order rather than demand order. Transport cycles are beginning to shift.

Red: First room entry is delayed past 7:30 a.m. EVS is receiving calls for rooms that were not on the morning sequence. Two or more techs are working the same zone, pulling rhythm from others. Transport has begun stacking requests. Placement is holding admits.

Engine 2: Transport Flow

Yellow: Moves are completing, but spacing is uneven. Two requests arrived within four minutes of each other. The next cycle has not started. Nursing on one unit received both admits in the same window. Response times are within range, but clustering has begun.

Red: Three or more requests are stacked simultaneously. Transport is completing moves but cannot get ahead of the queue. Nursing units are requesting holds. Placement is re-sequencing to relieve pressure. The ED has added a hold in the last 30 minutes.

Engine 3: Placement Flow

Yellow: Beds are being filled in order of availability rather than unit bandwidth. One unit is absorbing a disproportionate share of early admits. Placement is responding to the loudest request rather than sequencing by system load. No downstream capacity check has occurred in the last 20 minutes.

Red: One inpatient unit has requested a hold. Placement is making reactive decisions under pressure from the ED or PACU. Sequencing has broken down. The hospital is filling beds without a system view. Downstream units are beginning to compress.

Engine 4: Emergency Department Flow

Yellow: The ED board shows two or more patients waiting for inpatient beds placed more than 45 minutes ago. Bed confirmations are taking longer than usual. The charge nurse has made one informal escalation. No official hold has been called, but movement has slowed.

Red: Three or more patients are boarding with holds of 90 minutes or longer. The charge nurse has formally escalated. Triage is backing up. Hallway utilization has increased. The ED cannot receive the next wave without movement from upstream engines.

Engine 5: PACU Flow

Yellow: PACU cleared the first wave on time, but the second wave is arriving before first-wave patients have moved. One inpatient bed assigned to a PACU patient has not been confirmed. The OR completed its second case and the post-op destination is uncertain. No hold has been called, but the valve is narrowing.

Red: PACU is at capacity. One or more OR cases have been delayed because PACU cannot accept. Inpatient unit holds have been called. The surgical schedule is showing signs of compression. PACU leadership has escalated to house supervisor.

Engine 6: Inpatient Unit Flow

Yellow: Discharges are planned but have not been executed. Two or more patients are medically ready to leave but are waiting on orders, transport, or family. Admissions are arriving in pairs. Nursing bandwidth is tightening but not yet critical. No hold has been called.

Red: The unit has requested a hold on new admissions. Nursing is at ratio limit with active complex patients. Discharges are clustered in the afternoon rather than distributed through the morning. The unit cannot absorb additional pressure without a safety risk.

Why These Signals Matter

Yellow signals are quiet. They do not trigger dashboards. They do not justify escalation calls. That is precisely why they are dangerous. By the time every one of these engines shows Red simultaneously, the collapse has been building for hours.

The discipline is in acting at Yellow. Not because the outcome is certain, but because Yellow is the last moment when small corrections still work.

When these three disciplines slip:

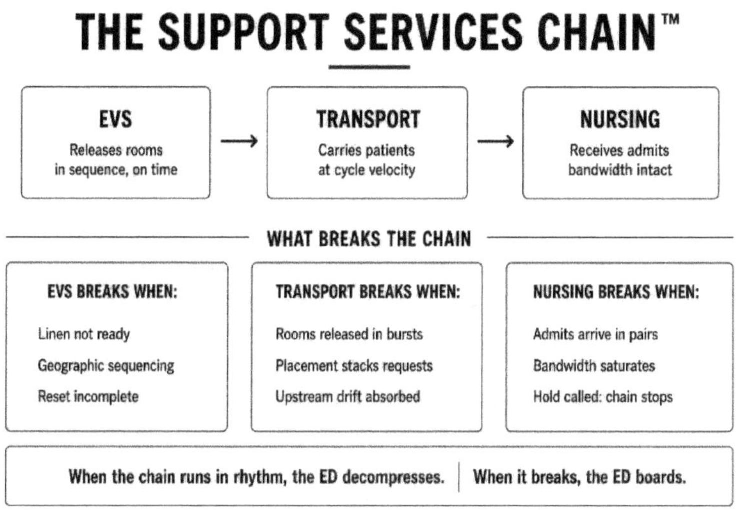

Figure 10: The Support Services Chain

- the Support Services Chain™ compresses
- ED boarding rises
- PACU density increases
- OR cases drift
- inpatient units become reactive
- leaders begin managing symptoms instead of flow

Drift doesn't begin with staffing or volume. It begins with missed signals, late timing, and incomplete readiness.

The Hidden Discipline in Practice: A Composite Case

> *At a 410-bed community health system, a house supervisor noticed that Yellow signals were routinely visible on the morning board but that no one was acting on them. Transport clustering appeared at 7:20 a.m. on most days. EVS room-release sequencing showed geographic batching rather than placement priority. The ED board began accumulating holds before 8:30 a.m. on the same days the clustering appeared.*

The supervisor began using the Yellow and Red signal matrix as a morning briefing tool. Rather than waiting for Red signals to trigger escalation, she built a standing 7:15 a.m. review of two data points: the first Transport request timestamp and the number of simultaneous EVS releases in the prior 30 minutes. Both were Yellow indicators for engines that were about to compress.

On days when clustering was Yellow at 7:15 a.m., she made one call to the placement coordinator to stagger the next two confirms by 12 minutes. That single small correction redistributed the Transport queue enough to prevent the burst absorption that had been producing ED holds by 9:00 a.m.

The correction took 90 seconds. The downstream effect was measurable within three weeks. On days when the Yellow correction was made, ED boarding before 10:00 a.m. declined by roughly half compared to days when it was not. No new staff were added. No initiative was launched. The discipline was in reading the signal early and making a small adjustment before the outcome was determined.

> *Composite scenario representing patterns observed across multiple hospital assessments.*

When these three disciplines hold:

- Engines start the day ahead.
- Placement matches sequence.
- Transport runs with rhythm.
- PACU clears first-wave patients.
- The OR stays on schedule.
- The ED decompresses early.
- Nursing receives admissions without compression.

Flow becomes predictable. Pressure becomes manageable. The hospital inherits calm instead of chaos.

Signals start the day. Timing protects the day. Readiness activates movement.

When they drift, every engine inherits collapse. When they align, every engine inherits flow.

The Support Services Chain

The engine chapters that follow show how the Support Services Chain™, EVS, Transport, and Placement, converts Signals, Timing, and Readiness into actual movement.

Next: Environmental Services (EVS)

If The Hidden Discipline defines what alignment looks like, EVS is where it is either confirmed or broken. Chapter 4 shows how the first visible engine of hospital flow either inherits readiness or absorbs drift it did not create.

CHAPTER 4

Engine 1: Environmental Services (EVS)

The First Visible Engine of Flow

The Morning That Started Before EVS Arrived

At 6:58 a.m., an EVS supervisor arrived on a medical-surgical floor to find the team already two rooms behind.

Nothing unusual had happened, no call-outs, no equipment failures.

The issue was upstream. The linen cart for the floor's high-turnover corridor had been stocked last the night before, with high-use items buried under low-priority stock. The first two rooms on the morning list required supplies from the bottom of the cart.

The team adapted. They reorganized the cart, retrieved supplies, and started cleaning.

Eleven minutes were lost before the first room was entered.

By 9:30 a.m., Transport had stacked requests, nursing absorbed simultaneous admissions, and the ED was holding a patient awaiting the third room for more than an hour.

No one traced the pressure back to 6:58 a.m.

The EVS team worked intensely. But they were compensating for a problem they didn't create.

The operational day does not begin with patients.

It begins with rooms.

Environmental Services is the first visible engine of hospital flow because it converts potential capacity into real capacity. Until EVS releases a room, nothing else can move.

- Transport cannot move.
- Placement cannot match.
- Nursing cannot receive.
- The ED cannot decompress.
- The OR cannot progress.

This is why EVS does more than support the hospital. EVS sets the pace of the entire day.

When EVS moves in rhythm, the hospital stabilizes early. When EVS drifts, every downstream engine absorbs the impact.

EVS is not downstream work. It is upstream control.

Why EVS Defines the Day

Hospitals experience flow as pressure or calm. That feeling is inherited.

EVS defines the hospital's rhythm because its early room releases determine:

- When the first admissions move.
- How Transport cycles begin.
- Whether Nursing receives patients evenly or in batches.

- Whether Placement can sequence with precision.
- Whether the ED decompresses early or holds.
- Whether surgical flow starts clean or compressed.

A ten-minute miss in EVS rarely stays ten minutes. It multiplies across the next several hours.

This is not because EVS is slow. It is because Flow Physics™ amplifies early timing errors.

The EVS Activation Window

Like every engine, EVS has an Activation Window, a short period early in the day when timing matters more than volume.

For most hospitals, this window sits within the first 60 to 90 minutes of the morning.

Inside this window, EVS determines whether the day runs ahead or behind.

If early rooms are released in sequence and on time, downstream engines find rhythm. If releases slip, downstream engines compress.

Once this window closes, the hospital spends the rest of the day reacting.

EVS does not just clean rooms during this window. EVS engineers the morning.

How Drift Starts in EVS

Drift rarely begins with a major failure. It begins quietly.

- A room starts out of sequence.
- A discharge clears later than expected.
- An isolation room takes longer than planned.
- An evening carryover steals a few morning minutes.
- A supply detour interrupts flow.

Individually, these moments feel insignificant. Collectively, they break rhythm.

Dashboards still look acceptable. Rooms still get cleaned. Staff still work hard.

But the physics are already broken.

For the Yellow and Red signals that mark where EVS drift becomes visible before it becomes a crisis, see the Yellow vs. Red Signal Matrix in Chapter 3.

The Seven-Minute Miss

At 7:42 a.m., an EVS technician entered a room scheduled for early release.

The linen cart was out of sequence. They detoured to another floor. Seven minutes were lost.

That seven-minute miss delayed Transport's first move.

Two admits stacked instead of spacing. Nursing received both during a high-workload moment. Placement lost sequencing rhythm. By mid-morning, the ED was holding patients.

No one blamed EVS. They blamed the ED.

This is how drift hides. Not loud. Not dramatic. Just early, and expensive.

EVS as the First Flow Chain

EVS does not operate in isolation.

It forms the hospital's first visible flow chain:

EVS releases → Transport moves → Nursing receives

This chain must run in rhythm.

When EVS releases rooms evenly, Transport maintains steady cycles. When Transport maintains rhythm, Nursing absorbs admits without compression. When Nursing stays balanced, downstream engines stabilize. When EVS drifts, the entire chain compensates, and pressure appears elsewhere.

What EVS Protects

EVS protects more than cleanliness. It protects:

- Timing.
- Sequence.
- Safety.
- Readiness.
- Predictability.

Accuracy matters not only because of standards, but because rework breaks timing. Broken timing breaks flow.

A room is either ready or not. Partial readiness is operational friction.

When EVS protects readiness, the hospital moves with confidence. When readiness is uncertain, the hospital hesitates.

The Role of Leadership in EVS Flow

EVS flow stabilizes when leaders protect the engine early.

Strong leaders:

- Round early.
- Enforce sequence.
- Correct drift immediately.
- Coordinate with Transport and Nursing.
- Protect the evening reset.
- Prevent small misses from multiplying.

Drift grows when leadership arrives late. Flow stabilizes when leadership intervenes early.

EVS and the Night Before

Tomorrow's flow is built the night before.

When evening EVS completes resets, clears carryover, and restores sequence, the morning starts ahead.

When evening EVS leaves unfinished work, the morning inherits pressure it cannot absorb.

The strongest EVS operations protect flow before the day begins.

EVS Rhythm in Practice: A Composite Case

In a 420-bed health system, EVS consistently received high productivity scores. Room turnaround times met benchmark targets. Yet mid-morning pressure was chronic.

An operational review revealed that while total room-clean times were acceptable, release sequencing was misaligned with placement demand. EVS was cleaning rooms in geographic order rather than in placement-priority order. High-demand rooms were frequently the last cleaned, not the first.

After restructuring morning room assignments to lead with placement-priority rooms and coordinating release timing with Transport's first-cycle window, the hospital's early admission rate moved from below benchmark to above it within the first thirty days. Placement coordinators reported fewer holds before 9:00 a.m. The change required no additional staff. The sequence adjustment was one of order: rooms were assigned by placement priority rather than geographic convenience.

Composite scenario representing patterns observed across multiple hospital assessments.

EVS is the first visible engine of hospital flow.

It doesn't just respond to demand; it shapes the day's operating rhythm.

When EVS holds rhythm, the hospital feels calm. When EVS drifts, the hospital spends the day compensating.

It makes readiness real, room by room, so the rest of the system can move.

Next: Transport Flow

Chapter 5 shows how Transport carries or loses the rhythm EVS establishes.

CHAPTER 5

Engine 2: Transport Flow

Where Readiness Becomes Movement

The Invisible Queue

At 8:14 a.m., a transport coordinator looked at her board and saw four pending requests, all submitted within a six-minute window.

Nothing had gone wrong that morning. No staff shortages. No equipment issues. The team was performing.

But EVS had released three rooms simultaneously after a brief supply delay. Placement had sequenced two additional admits in response to early ED pressure. Five requests arrived in a cluster.

The transport team moved quickly. But a team that averages 2.4 moves per hour under normal sequencing was now absorbing a burst that required four moves in 20 minutes.

The math didn't work.

Two patients waited over 35 minutes. Nursing absorbed the delay. The ED board added a third hold.

No one expected Transport to fail. Transport absorbed an upstream timing problem, and revealed it downstream.

EVS creates readiness. Transport turns readiness into movement.

Without Transport, readiness sits idle. Without rhythm, readiness becomes congestion.

Transport is not a support function. It is the engine that carries rhythm across the hospital.

When Transport moves in sequence, flow spreads smoothly. When Transport drifts, every engine downstream feels compression.

Transport does not just move patients. It decides whether time is spent in rhythm or in recovery.

Transport Is a Velocity Engine, Not a Speed Engine

Speed is how fast a single move occurs. Velocity is how predictably moves repeat.

Hospitals rarely fail because Transport is slow. They fail because Transport is uneven.

- When moves cluster, Nursing compresses.
- When moves stall, EVS backs up.
- When moves surge, Placement loses sequence.
- When moves drift, the ED holds.

Transport stability is not about racing. It is about spacing.

Transport Inherits, It Does Not Control

Transport does not control:

- When rooms are ready.

- When patients discharge.
- When admissions are ready.
- When PACU releases.
- When the ED needs relief.

Transport inherits all of it.

This is why Transport often appears overwhelmed even when teams are working hard. They are absorbing upstream timing decisions made elsewhere.

Transport is not failing when it feels busy. It is revealing misalignment upstream.

The Transport Activation Window

Like EVS, Transport has an Activation Window.

This window begins the moment the first rooms are released and the first admits are ready to move.

During this window, Transport determines whether:

- Movement starts evenly or in bursts.
- Nursing receives patients steadily or in waves.
- Placement maintains sequence or reacts.
- The ED decompresses or holds.
- PACU clears space or fills.

When Transport establishes early rhythm, the day stabilizes. When Transport misses the window, the hospital spends hours compensating.

Transport does not recover rhythm easily once compression sets in. It carries momentum forward, good or bad.

How Transport Drift Forms

Transport drift rarely announces itself. It forms when:

- Early moves are delayed and then batch.
- Assignments stack instead of spacing.
- One late move cascades into several.
- Upstream releases arrive unevenly.
- Downstream units cannot receive on time.

Transport teams still move patients. Moves still complete. Metrics may still look acceptable.

But rhythm is gone.

Drift does not look like failure. It looks like effort without relief.

For the Yellow and Red signals that distinguish manageable Transport clustering from full burst absorption, see the Yellow vs. Red Signal Matrix in Chapter 3.

Transport as the Connective Engine

Transport sits between every major engine:

- EVS
- Nursing
- Placement
- ED
- PACU
- OR

Because of this, Transport carries more system stress than any other engine.

When upstream engines align, Transport feels calm. When upstream engines drift, Transport absorbs friction from all sides.

Transport is not the cause of congestion. It is the conduit through which congestion travels.

The Staffing Trap: Why Adding Transport Doesn't Hold

Hospitals that expand transport teams in response to chronic delays consistently see the same result across operational assessments: temporary improvement followed by the same pressure returning within months. The resource was not the constraint.

Flow improves when:

- EVS releases rooms evenly.
- Placement sequences intelligently.
- Nursing can receive without compression.
- PACU clears in rhythm.
- ED admissions move early.

When these conditions exist, Transport naturally stabilizes.

When they do not, Transport becomes the visible bottleneck, even though the cause lives elsewhere.

Transport is not a capacity problem. It is a coordination problem.

This holds even when the tools are identical. Across eight sites within one regional health system, operating the same technology, the same 30-minute turnaround goal, and the same operational framework, actual performance ranged from 18 to 47 minutes, and only two of the eight consistently met the goal. The difference was not the system. It was execution.

What Disciplined Transport Leadership Looks Like

Transport discipline is not about moving faster. It is about maintaining even spacing under pressure and catching clustering before it cascades.

A transport coordinator practicing upstream discipline watches not just the current request but the pattern of requests. When two requests arrive within three minutes of each other, that coordinator communicates immediately with placement: the next release should be spaced, not immediate. That single communication prevents the third request from arriving before the first two are resolved.

Transport leaders protect the morning window by treating it differently from the rest of the day. The first 90 minutes of Transport activity set the rhythm for everything that follows. A coordinator who holds early spacing firm, even when ED pressure pushes for faster placement, gives the system a foundation it will draw on through noon.

The strongest Transport operations also manage the idle window. When burst absorption creates a 20-minute gap in requests, that window is not downtime. It is recovery capacity. Protecting it rather than filling it with non-essential moves allows the engine to be ready for the next wave without carrying forward the compression of the last one.

How Transport Reveals System Health

Because Transport sits between every major engine, its behavior is one of the most reliable indicators of system alignment. Leaders who watch Transport are watching the whole hospital.

On aligned days, Transport requests arrive in a steady, manageable sequence. Individual moves complete in predictable windows. Coordinators are not escalating. Nursing is not calling for holds. The board is clear. These are not lucky days. They are the product of upstream engines operating in rhythm.

On drifted days, the pattern is unmistakable before the ED announces it. Requests cluster. Response windows lengthen. Coordinators begin improvising. The language of the team shifts from coordination to management. These signals, visible in Transport before they are visible anywhere else in the system, are early correction opportunities that most hospitals miss because no one is watching Transport with that lens.

The leader who watches Transport velocity at 7:30 a.m. knows what the ED board will look like at 9:30 a.m. That is the value of the engine-as-indicator mindset. Transport does not just carry patients. It carries a real-time picture of upstream alignment.

Transport and Flow Perception

Leaders often experience Transport issues as "communication problems."

In reality, they are timing problems.

- Late notifications.
- Urgent pages.
- Competing priorities.

These are not failures of communication. They are symptoms of misaligned engines creating urgency.

Transport feels the escalation first.

Transport Rhythm in Practice: A Composite Case

A 600-bed academic medical center had expanded its transport team twice in three years in response to chronic delays. Response times improved temporarily after each expansion. Within six months, pressure returned.

An operational analysis found that the issue was not staffing, it was release clustering. EVS was releasing rooms in geographic batches rather than staggered sequences. Placement was confirming admits in clusters tied to rounding patterns. Transport was absorbing bursts of 4–5 simultaneous requests, then experiencing 20–25 minute idle windows.

After coordinating EVS release sequencing with Transport scheduling and introducing staggered placement confirmation windows, Transport's move distribution became more even. Patient wait times declined. Staffing levels were unchanged. The sequence adjustment was one of timing distribution: staggered release and confirmation windows replaced burst-driven dispatch.

> *Composite scenario representing patterns observed across multiple hospital assessments.*

Transport does not create flow. Transport carries it.

When readiness is released evenly, Transport spreads rhythm across the hospital. When readiness arrives unevenly, Transport amplifies compression.

Next: Placement Flow

If Transport moves patients, Placement decides where movement lands.

Placement determines whether movement creates stability or chaos.

Chapter 6 shows how Placement sequencing protects flow or breaks it, long before patients arrive at the bedside.

CHAPTER 6

Engine 3: Placement Flow

Where Movement Becomes Stability or Chaos

The Admit That Tipped the Unit

At 10:22 a.m., a placement coordinator received a call from the ED requesting an urgent admit for a patient who had been boarding for four hours.

Two beds were open. One was on a unit already running at high census with a charge nurse managing a complex admission. The other was on a quieter unit with more bandwidth.

The coordinator placed the patient in the open bed closest to the ED elevator. Faster. Simpler. The right call for one patient.

Within 40 minutes, the receiving unit requested a hold on further admits. Twenty minutes later, a second complex patient arrived from PACU to the same unit. By noon, the unit was operationally saturated, and two more ED patients waited more than 90 minutes for placement.

The bed was open. The sequence was wrong.

Placement is not about filling beds. Placement is about protecting balance.

Placement is not an administrative function. It is a sequencing engine.

When Placement aligns patients into the system correctly, flow smooths downstream. When Placement drifts, movement turns into congestion, even when every other engine is performing well.

Placement does not move patients. Placement determines where pressure lands.

Placement Is a Sequencing Engine

Speed does not protect flow. Sequence does.

Placement controls sequence by deciding:

- Which patient goes next.
- Where they go.
- When they move.
- What downstream load that decision creates.

Two patients placed into the wrong order can create more disruption than ten placed correctly.

Placement is where balance is protected or broken.

Why Placement Feels Invisible, Until It Fails

When Placement works well, no one notices. Patients move. Units receive. The ED decompresses. PACU clears.

When Placement fails, everyone feels it. Nursing compresses. Transport surges. EVS scrambles. ED holds rise. OR cases stall.

Placement does not create problems loudly. It creates them quietly, by breaking sequence.

Placement Inherits Pressure, Then Redistributes It

Placement inherits pressure from:

- ED admits
- PACU releases
- Direct admits
- Transfers
- Delayed discharges

Placement cannot eliminate pressure. It can only distribute it.

Correct distribution stabilizes the system. Poor distribution concentrates pressure and creates failure points.

Placement is where upstream stress becomes downstream reality.

The Placement Activation Window

Like EVS and Transport, Placement has an Activation Window.

This window opens when the first ready beds appear and the first admits are waiting.

During this window, Placement determines whether:

- Admits arrive spaced or stacked.
- Nursing units absorb evenly or compress.
- Transport flows or surges.

- ED holding clears or persists.
- PACU creates space or backs up.

Early sequence decisions compound quickly.

Once poor sequence is established, the hospital spends the day correcting instead of flowing.

Placement cannot outrun early mis-sequencing.

How Placement Drift Forms

Placement drift rarely looks like a mistake. It forms when:

- Urgency overrides sequence.
- The loudest request wins.
- Short-term relief overrides system balance.
- One exception becomes precedent.
- Downstream capacity is assumed instead of confirmed.

Each decision feels reasonable in isolation. Together, they destabilize the system.

Placement drift is not a judgment problem. It is a physics problem.

For the Yellow and Red signals that mark where Placement is sequencing reactively rather than by system load, see the Yellow vs. Red Signal Matrix in Chapter 3.

Placement as the Load Balancer

Placement determines not just where patients go, but how much stress each unit absorbs.

Balanced placement:

- protects nursing bandwidth
- preserves Transport rhythm
- prevents EVS rework
- allows ED decompression
- keeps PACU flowing

Unbalanced placement:

- overloads specific units
- forces batch movement
- creates staffing stress
- increases handoff risk
- triggers reactive leadership

Placement decides where the system bends, and where it breaks.

Why "Fill the Open Bed" Breaks Flow

Open beds are not interchangeable.

Beds differ by:

- staffing readiness
- acuity tolerance
- unit bandwidth

- timing context

Filling the first open bed without sequence consideration feels efficient. It often creates downstream compression.

Placement protects flow when it treats beds as contextual capacity, not empty space.

Sequence matters more than speed.

Placement and Flow Perception

Leaders often experience Placement problems as:

- staffing issues
- communication breakdowns
- nursing resistance
- transport delays

In reality, these are secondary effects.

When sequence holds, communication quiets. When sequence breaks, urgency escalates.

Placement feels stressful not because it is difficult, but because it absorbs pressure from every direction.

What Sequencing by Bandwidth Actually Means

Most placement coordinators are trained to find an open bed. The bandwidth-aware coordinator asks a different question: which bed, in which unit, with which staffing context, can absorb this patient right now without compressing that unit's ability to receive the next one?

That question requires three pieces of information that go beyond bed availability. The first is current admit activity on each unit. A unit with two beds open but three recent admissions in the last 90 minutes is not as available as it appears. Those nurses are still orienting new patients. Their cognitive bandwidth is compressed even when their physical beds are open.

The second is acuity tolerance at this moment. A unit running a high-acuity patient population during the morning hours may technically have a standard bed available for a lower-acuity patient. But the staffing is oriented toward complex care. The admission workflow is stretched. Adding a standard patient to that unit during peak complexity is not the relief it appears to be.

The third is discharge timing on adjacent units. If an adjacent unit has three anticipated discharges in the next 45 minutes, the bandwidth picture changes significantly. A coordinator who knows that will hold the next admit for that unit rather than stacking it onto the already-compressed unit. That 45-minute patience protects both units and keeps the system flowing.

The Placement Decision as a System Act

Every placement decision is a system act, not a unit act. This distinction is the hardest shift for placement coordinators to make because the pressure they receive is local. The ED charge nurse is calling. The PACU nurse is escalating. The pressure is specific and urgent.

The discipline is to respond to that urgency with a system response rather than a unit response. Not: which bed is open. But: which placement decision protects system flow for the next two hours.

Hospitals that train placement coordinators to think this way produce a noticeable downstream effect. ED holds drop. Transport rhythm stabilizes. Nursing units report more even admission distribution. None of this requires more staff. It requires a different decision framework applied consistently by one coordinator with system-level visibility.

Placement Sequencing in Practice: A Composite Case

> *At a 375-bed regional hospital, nursing directors on two units consistently reported higher-than-average patient-to-nurse ratios during the late morning. Other units on the same floor reported lighter loads at the same time. Census appeared balanced on paper.*

A placement audit revealed a sequencing pattern: placement coordinators were routing admits to the units with the fastest bed turnaround times, regardless of current unit bandwidth. Units that turned rooms quickly received disproportionate early-morning volume.

After introducing a bandwidth-adjusted placement protocol that factored in current admit activity, staffing ratios, and acuity load, not just bed availability, the two chronically compressed units saw measurable improvement in admission spacing. Staff reported a noticeable reduction in early-morning pressure. The sequence adjustment was one of criteria: placement decisions were restructured around unit bandwidth rather than bed availability.

> *Composite scenario representing patterns observed across multiple hospital assessments.*

Placement does not move patients. Placement decides how movement lands.

Readiness. Motion. Balance.

Next: Emergency Department Flow

The ED does not create flow problems. It reveals them.

Chapter 7 shows how ED pressure reflects the alignment or misalignment of every upstream engine.

CHAPTER 7

Engine 4: Emergency Department Flow

The Hospital's Early Warning System

The Board That Told the Truth

At 11:15 a.m., the ED charge nurse escalated to the house supervisor.

Twelve patients were waiting for inpatient beds. Six had been boarding for more than two hours. Three more were in triage.

Leadership pulled the staffing report. Adequate. They checked the census report. Beds were available on three floors.

"Why aren't these patients moving?"

The answer was not in the ED.

Two of the available beds had not been released by EVS due to a morning supply issue. Three beds were confirmed available but the receiving units had not acknowledged readiness signals. Placement had sequenced four additional admits from surgery without coordinating with ED hold status.

The ED board was not showing an ED problem.

It was showing the accumulated result of four upstream timing gaps that had been compounding since 7:30 a.m.

The ED did not cause the surge. The ED reported it.

The ED does not create flow problems. It reveals them.

The ED is where upstream misalignment becomes visible first, not because the ED is weak, but because it sits at the point of highest exposure.

When upstream engines are aligned, the ED feels calm. When they drift, the ED absorbs pressure immediately.

The ED is the hospital's early warning system.

Why the ED Feels Pressure First

The ED sits at the intersection of:

- Unpredictable arrivals.
- Fixed physical space.
- Immediate demand.
- Downstream dependency.

It has no buffer.

When EVS releases rooms evenly, pressure dissipates. When Transport carries rhythm forward, movement spreads. When Placement sequences correctly, balance holds.

When any of these break, the ED feels it first, and longest.

ED congestion is not a failure of response. It is the visible symptom of upstream drift.

The ED Does Not Control Absorption

The ED does not decide:

- When beds become ready.

- When admissions move.
- When PACU clears.
- When inpatient units receive.
- When placement sequence holds.

The ED absorbs whatever the system delivers.

This is why ED teams often feel like they are running harder without relief. They are compensating for timing decisions made elsewhere.

Arrivals Are Predictable, Absorption Is Not

ED arrivals follow patterns. They rise. They fall. They repeat.

Chaos does not come from arrivals. It comes from blocked exits.

When admits move steadily, the ED flows, even on busy days. When admits stall, the ED backs up, even on average days.

ED flow is governed by outflow, not inflow.

The effect is measurable. A multi-hospital academic medical system documented an average ED occupied time of 79 minutes before reworking its operations. Over four years of workflow optimization, including automated dispatch of patient transport, that figure fell to 52 minutes system-wide, with the transport component reaching 25 to 28 minutes, below the published national benchmark of 30.

The ED as a Pressure Amplifier

Pressure does not remain localized in the ED.

When ED holds increase:

- Triage compresses.
- Hallway utilization rises.
- Decision velocity slows.
- Staffing strain escalates.
- Downstream engines feel urgency.

The ED does not create this pressure. It amplifies it so leaders can no longer ignore it.

This is why ED distress feels sudden. It isn't sudden. It is accumulated.

The ED Activation Window

Like every engine, the ED has an Activation Window.

This window opens early, often before leaders arrive.

During this period, the ED's trajectory for the day is largely set by:

- early room readiness
- transport rhythm
- placement sequencing
- inpatient reception capacity

If early admits move, the ED decompresses. If they do not, pressure compounds.

Once ED holding reaches a critical mass, recovery becomes difficult. The ED does not reset easily.

Why ED "Surges" Are Misunderstood

ED surges are often described as sudden or unavoidable.

In reality, most surges are inherited. They form when:

- Early movement is delayed.
- Releases cluster instead of spacing.
- Placement concentrates load.
- Downstream units cannot receive.
- Transport loses rhythm.

By the time the surge is visible in the ED, the causative decisions are hours old.

The ED did not surge. The system did.

For the Yellow and Red signals that distinguish early ED pressure from full boarding crisis, see the Yellow vs. Red Signal Matrix in Chapter 3.

The ED and Surgical Flow

The ED often reflects surgical misalignment before surgery notices it.

When PACU fills:

- Surgical admissions slow.
- Inpatient beds remain occupied.
- ED admissions stall.

- ED holding rises.

The ED becomes the spillover point for surgical timing drift.

This is why ED pressure frequently coincides with "on-time" OR schedules. The schedule held. The system did not.

Why the ED Cannot Fix Itself

Fast-track lanes, triage redesigns, dedicated admission nurses. Hospitals have tried them all. They improve the experience inside the ED. They rarely reduce boarding, because boarding is not an ED problem. It is a system timing problem that surfaces in the ED.

Flow stabilizes when:

- EVS releases rooms in rhythm.
- Transport carries movement evenly.
- Placement protects sequence.
- Inpatient units absorb consistently.
- PACU clears predictably.

When these engines align, ED pressure fades without intervention.

The ED does not need fixing. The system does.

ED Flow in Practice: A Composite Case

A 450-bed health system had invested significantly in ED-specific interventions over two years: fast-track redesign, triage protocols, and a dedicated admission nurse. Patient satisfaction scores improved. Boarding times remained persistently elevated.

An upstream flow analysis revealed that 74 percent of boarding events occurred on days when First Movement Time™ exceeded 7:50 a.m. On those same days, EVS room release sequencing was consistently misaligned with placement priority. Transport experienced morning request clustering on those days at a rate 2.3 times higher than low-boarding days. These operational findings are consistent with published research. A 2024 study in the Annals of Emergency Medicine using time-driven activity-based costing methodology found that boarding patients in emergency departments nearly doubles the daily cost of care per patient. Separately, peer-reviewed financial modeling published in the Annals of Emergency Medicine documented that hospitals using dynamic bed management strategies to reduce ED boarding stood to recover $2.7 to $3.6 million annually in net revenue at a single inner-city teaching hospital, figures the authors described as the result of optimal dynamic policies, not static or partial interventions. The mechanism is not staffing additions. It is upstream flow correction.

The ED had not been the problem. It had been the indicator. When upstream sequencing was stabilized, boarding times declined without any additional ED-specific intervention. The sequence adjustment happened entirely upstream: release sequencing and Transport timing were corrected before the ED ever became the focus.

Composite scenario representing patterns observed across multiple hospital assessments.

The ED does not break the hospital. The hospital breaks the ED.

When upstream engines align, the ED becomes calm, controlled, and predictable.

When they drift, the ED becomes the first alarm.

ED flow is not an emergency problem. It is a system timing problem.

The ED does not lie. It reports.

Next: PACU Flow

If the ED is the early warning system, PACU is the pressure valve.

PACU determines whether surgical flow holds or backs up into every other engine.

Chapter 8 shows how PACU absorbs upstream timing, and either protects the surgical schedule or exposes its failure.

CHAPTER 8

Engine 5: PACU Flow

Where Surgical Timing Holds, or Collapses

The On-Time Case That Stalled the Schedule

At 9:47 a.m., the third surgical case of the day finished on time.

The OR team documented completion. The schedule was holding.

But PACU had not released the first two patients from the morning wave. Both were medically ready, and both had been ready for more than 30 minutes.

Their assigned inpatient beds were not confirmed. One was still occupied. One was clean but not released in the system.

The third patient arrived in PACU and joined the queue.

By 10:30 a.m., PACU was at capacity. The fourth case was closing. The OR held.

The schedule was on time. The system was not.

The OR did not fail. Upstream engines failed to clear the path.

PACU does not exist to recover patients. It exists to protect flow.

PACU sits between two powerful forces:

- The surgical schedule pushing patients forward.
- Inpatient capacity pulling patients through.

When those forces are aligned, PACU is calm. When they are not, PACU becomes the point of compression.

PACU does not create pressure. It contains it, until it cannot.

PACU Is a Release Engine

Every engine upstream has fed into this moment. The ED revealed the system's condition. PACU determines whether surgery can continue. PACU determines whether surgical flow holds.

PACU is not an inflow problem. It is a release problem.

When PACU releases patients predictably, surgery stays on time. When PACU stalls, the schedule fractures.

PACU does not control the volume it receives. It controls how long pressure is held.

Why PACU Feels Calm, Until It Doesn't

PACU often appears stable right up until the moment it fills.

This is because pressure accumulates quietly.

PACU absorbs:

- Delayed discharges.
- Uneven bed readiness.
- Transport drift.
- Placement mis-sequencing.

- Surgical punctuality without downstream capacity.

When release slows, PACU does not immediately fail. It compresses.

For the Yellow and Red signals that mark where PACU is narrowing before it stalls, see the Yellow vs. Red Signal Matrix in Chapter 3.

The PACU Activation Window

Like every engine, PACU has an Activation Window.

This window opens early in the surgical day, often between the first and second operative waves.

During this period, PACU determines whether:

- Early cases clear cleanly.
- OR momentum holds.
- Downstream units absorb evenly.
- Pressure dissipates or compounds.

If PACU clears the first wave smoothly, the schedule stabilizes. If it does not, compression cascades through the day.

PACU does not regain lost rhythm easily. Once the valve sticks, pressure builds.

PACU and the Illusion of "On-Time" Surgery

Operating rooms can run on time while the system falls behind.

When PACU release slows:

- OR cases pause.
- Holding increases.
- Downstream beds remain occupied.
- ED admissions stall.
- pressure spreads

PACU exposes the difference between procedural punctuality and system readiness.

The Capacity Illusion: What More PACU Space Actually Buys

An extra bay buys time. It does not buy alignment. If the downstream beds are not ready and inpatient units cannot receive, additional PACU space fills at the same rate as the original. The valve gets larger. The pressure behind it does not change.

PACU stabilizes when:

- inpatient beds are released early
- EVS holds rhythm
- Transport carries movement evenly
- Placement sequences intelligently
- downstream units receive predictably

When these engines align, PACU remains open. When they drift, PACU absorbs pressure until it spills back.

PACU as the Pressure Valve

Every system needs a valve. PACU is the hospital's.

When pressure is released steadily, flow holds. When pressure is trapped, failure propagates.

PACU does not cause delays. It reveals whether the system can release what surgery produces.

What the PACU-Surgical Relationship Actually Requires

The operating room and PACU are typically managed as a single surgical service line, and yet they operate on fundamentally different timing assumptions. The OR is optimized for case start times and procedural efficiency. PACU is optimized for patient stability and discharge readiness. These two optimization goals conflict the moment inpatient capacity is not available to receive PACU patients.

The root of most PACU holds is not a PACU problem. It is an upstream sequencing problem that manifests in PACU because PACU is the last point of holding before OR throughput is directly affected. By the time PACU holds impact OR cases, the failure is already hours old.

What the PACU-surgical relationship requires is not faster PACU discharge. It requires confirmed downstream readiness before surgical cases begin. The 8:45 a.m. bed confirmation protocol is one version of this. The principle behind it is straightforward: the OR should not start the second wave until PACU has a confirmed downstream exit for the first wave. This is not a PACU rule. It is a system rule that happens to be enforced at the PACU level.

What Strong PACU Leadership Protects

PACU leaders who protect flow think in waves, not in individual patients. The question is not whether this patient is ready to move. The question is whether the first wave has a clear exit before the second wave fills the unit.

Strong PACU leadership communicates upstream and downstream simultaneously. Upstream means flagging to the OR coordinator when PACU census is building and the next wave cannot be absorbed without confirmed downstream exits. Downstream means communicating directly with inpatient unit charge nurses and placement at defined thresholds, not waiting for the situation to become critical.

The PACU that waits until it is full before escalating has already lost the correction window. The PACU that communicates at 60 percent capacity, when there is still time to sequence exits, holds the surgical schedule intact. That communication habit is the difference between a day that runs and a day that stalls at noon. The operational cost of failing to act early is measurable. A 2024 study in Perioperative Care and Operating Room Management found that PACU boarding beyond four hours is associated with approximately 14 percent higher direct care costs and a statistically significant increase in total hospital length of stay across elective orthopedic and spine procedures. The cause in every case was the same: a mismatch between PACU throughput and downstream inpatient bed availability. The solution in every case was upstream, not in the PACU, but in the sequencing decisions made hours earlier.

The asymmetry is worth naming. A post-surgical recovery bay is among the most resource-intensive spaces in the hospital, far more so than an emergency department bed. The most expensive beds in the hospital are often the ones patients wait in longest.

PACU does not control whether upstream engines deliver on time. It controls how long it holds pressure before that pressure spills backward. The discipline is in releasing pressure steadily rather than holding it until the valve breaks.

PACU Flow in Practice: A Composite Case

> *At a 300-bed surgical hospital, OR on-time starts consistently exceeded 85 percent. Yet surgical cases routinely ran late in the afternoon, and OR leadership frequently cited PACU holds as the cause.*

A flow analysis traced the holds to a recurring pattern: inpatient beds assigned to first-wave PACU patients were not being confirmed as ready until after 9:30 a.m. By then, the second surgical wave was already adding patients to PACU. The valve was stuck before the second wave even began.

After introducing an 8:45 a.m. bed confirmation protocol that required inpatient unit readiness acknowledgment before the first PACU patient was transported, hold times dropped, falling below their pre-protocol baseline within the first thirty days. The OR ran its first on-time afternoon completion in the same week. The sequence adjustment was one of confirmation timing: downstream readiness was verified before surgical cases closed, not after.

> *Composite scenario representing patterns observed across multiple hospital assessments.*

PACU does not run the surgical day. It proves whether the surgical day can run.

When upstream engines align, PACU is quiet, controlled, and invisible. When they do not, PACU becomes the breaking point everyone feels.

What PACU cannot do is hide. When the system is aligned, PACU is the quietest room in the hospital. When it is not, PACU is the first place you feel it.

Next: Inpatient Unit Flow

If PACU is the pressure valve, inpatient units are the final absorbers.

They determine whether released patients become stability, or return pressure back upstream.

The Inpatient Unit Flow chapter that follows shows how inpatient unit flow completes the system, or collapses it.

CHAPTER 9

Engine 6: Inpatient Unit Flow

Where Pressure Is Absorbed, or Sent Back Upstream

The Unit That Could Not Receive

At 1:14 p.m., three patients were waiting for beds on 7 North.

The unit had two confirmed open beds. Census appeared manageable. Staffing was within ratio.

But 7 North had received five admissions between 9:00 and 11:30 a.m., three of them complex. The charge nurse was managing two simultaneous care plans, a family meeting, and a patient requiring isolation precautions.

The unit was not full. The unit was saturated.

Accepting three more patients in the next 90 minutes was operationally impossible without a safety compromise.

The charge nurse requested a hold.

Placement escalated. Transport waited. The ED added three more holds. PACU flagged a potential surgical delay.

The system had not run out of beds. It had run out of bandwidth.

Inpatient units do not end flow. They absorb it.

Every patient the hospital moves eventually arrives here.

What happens next determines whether pressure dissolves, or returns upstream.

Inpatient units are not destinations. They are absorbers.

When inpatient flow holds, the system stabilizes. When it breaks, pressure rebounds into every engine that came before it.

Inpatient Units Are Not Capacity, They Are Bandwidth

Beds existing does not mean beds are usable.

Inpatient flow is governed by bandwidth, not inventory.

Bandwidth is shaped by:

- timing of discharges
- admission spacing
- nursing load balance
- handoff rhythm
- environmental readiness

A unit with empty beds but compressed bandwidth cannot absorb flow. A unit with fewer beds but stable rhythm often can.

Inpatient units do not fail because beds are full. They fail because bandwidth is saturated.

Why Inpatient Units Feel Stable, Until They Don't

Inpatient pressure builds quietly. Units absorb:

- uneven admissions
- late discharges

- stacked transfers
- PACU releases without spacing
- ED admits without sequence

At first, staff compensate. Work stretches. Priorities shift.

Eventually, absorption capacity is exceeded.

When that happens:

- admits slow
- releases delay
- beds lock
- upstream engines stall

The unit did not fail suddenly. It absorbed pressure until it couldn't.

For the Yellow and Red signals that distinguish a unit absorbing pressure from a unit unable to receive, see the Yellow vs. Red Signal Matrix in Chapter 3.

The Inpatient Activation Window

Like every engine, inpatient units have an Activation Window.

This window opens early, when the first discharges should occur and the first admits arrive.

During this period, inpatient units determine whether:

- discharges free capacity on time
- admissions are absorbed evenly

- PACU can release
- ED admits can move
- upstream pressure dissipates

When early discharges hold, the system breathes. When they slip, the system compresses.

Inpatient units cannot easily recover from missed early releases. Lost capacity compounds across the day.

How Pressure Returns Upstream

When inpatient absorption slows:

- PACU fills
- OR cases pause
- ED admits stall
- Transport surges
- EVS rework increases

This rebound is not a failure of upstream engines. It is the natural consequence of blocked absorption.

Inpatient units are the final gate. When the gate holds, pressure backs up everywhere else.

Why Discharge Planning Does Not Solve Flow

Discharge planning improves outcomes. It does not guarantee flow.

Flow depends on when discharges occur, not whether they exist.

- Late discharges still consume bandwidth.
- Clustered discharges still compress absorption.
- Unpredictable discharges still destabilize sequencing.

Inpatient flow stabilizes when discharge timing is reliable, not when plans are complete.

The scale of this hidden loss is easy to underestimate. At one institution in a single year, 6,577 of 32,884 discharged patients had their departure times backdated, corrected after the fact because the patient was still physically in the bed when the discharge order was entered. The average hold per backdated discharge was 54 minutes. Added together, backdating alone produced 246.6 days of dead bedtime in a single year, capacity that existed on paper but never moved.

Inpatient Units and the Illusion of Local Optimization

Units often optimize locally to survive pressure.

That optimization can look like:

- delaying admissions
- batching movement
- protecting internal workflow
- resisting upstream urgency

Each choice feels rational. Collectively, they destabilize the system.

Local optimization does not protect flow. System absorption does.

The Inpatient Unit as the System Completer

Every engine before inpatient units prepares pressure for absorption.

- EVS creates readiness.
- Transport creates motion.
- Placement creates balance.
- The ED reveals misalignment.
- PACU releases surgical pressure.
- Inpatient units decide whether all of that effort resolves or rebounds.

They complete the system.

The Discharge Timing Architecture

The single highest-leverage operational change available to most inpatient units is not staffing, not communication, and not technology. It is the architecture of discharge timing. When discharges are distributed across the morning rather than clustered in the afternoon, the entire hospital breathes differently.

The mechanics are simple. A hospital with 40 anticipated discharges on a given day that executes 30 percent of them before 11:00 a.m. creates 12 beds of absorption capacity during the morning window. Those 12 beds allow Transport to keep moving, allow Placement to sequence without holding, allow PACU to release first-wave patients, and allow the ED to decompress before boarding accumulates. No new staff are required. The capacity existed all along. Only the timing changed.

Achieving morning discharges requires three things that most hospitals have not consistently built. The first is clinical decision-making completed the evening before. Discharge orders should not require morning rounds to initiate. For patients anticipated to leave the following day, orders should be entered the night before contingent on morning confirmation. This shifts the bottleneck from physician availability at 10:00 a.m. to a 10-minute confirmation window at 7:30 a.m.

The second is patient and family education completed the day before discharge. Families who receive discharge teaching at 8:00 p.m. the night before are ready to leave at 9:00 a.m. the next morning. Families who receive discharge teaching at 10:00 a.m. on the day of discharge are not leaving until 2:00 p.m. The education is not the bottleneck. The timing of the education is.

The third is transportation and social work coordination completed before morning. The most common reason an early discharge does not happen early is a transportation gap discovered at the last moment. A unit that routinely checks discharge logistics the afternoon before removes the surprise entirely.

Why Inpatient Units Are the System's Final Argument

Every chapter before this one described engines that set up, carry, and direct flow. Inpatient units are where all of that investment is either validated or wasted. A hospital can have perfect linen sequencing, excellent EVS rhythm, disciplined Transport, intelligent Placement, a calm ED, and a clear PACU. But if inpatient units cannot absorb predictably, none of it produces the outcome the system was designed to create.

This is why inpatient unit leaders carry an unusual burden. They are the recipients of every upstream success and every upstream failure simultaneously. When the system runs well, patients arrive spaced appropriately and nurses can care for them well. When the system drifts, nurses absorb the consequences of decisions made hours earlier by people they never saw.

Understanding this changes how inpatient unit leaders see their role. They are not simply managing their unit. They are completing the system. And the system completes well or poorly depending on whether inpatient leaders protect two things: discharge timing and admission sequencing. When those hold, the hospital flows. When they drift, the hospital churns, regardless of how well every other engine performed.

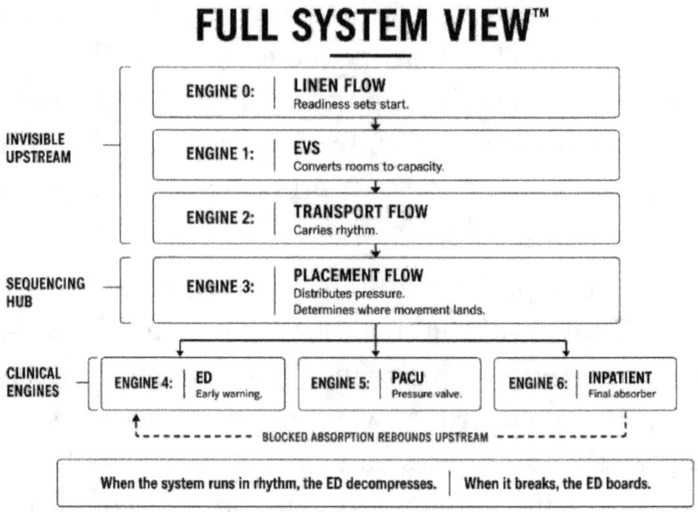

Figure 11: The Full System View

Inpatient Flow in Practice: A Composite Case

> *At a 520-bed medical center, leaders noted that despite strong discharge planning metrics, the hospital consistently experienced afternoon capacity crises. Discharge completion rates were above 90 percent by 3:00 p.m. Yet ED boarding and PACU holds were chronic from late morning onward.*

The problem was timing, not volume. More than 65 percent of discharges were occurring between 1:00 and 3:00 p.m. Inpatient bandwidth was saturated during the morning admission window when most surgical and ED admits were expected.

After piloting an early discharge incentive protocol on two units, targeting 30 percent of anticipated discharges before 11:00 a.m., morning absorption capacity improved measurably. PACU holds declined in the same period. The afternoon crisis pattern became less frequent. The sequence adjustment was one of discharge timing: the architecture of when discharges occurred was redesigned to relieve the morning admission window, not the afternoon.

> *Composite scenario representing patterns observed across multiple hospital assessments.*

Inpatient units do not end flow. They prove whether flow can end.

When inpatient units absorb pressure predictably, the hospital feels calm. When they cannot, the hospital churns.

Inpatient flow is not a unit problem. It is the final expression of system timing.

The hospital does not move faster than its inpatient units can absorb.

Now that every engine has been revealed, the question is no longer where flow breaks.

It is why the system tolerates drift, and how leaders can see it early enough to prevent it.

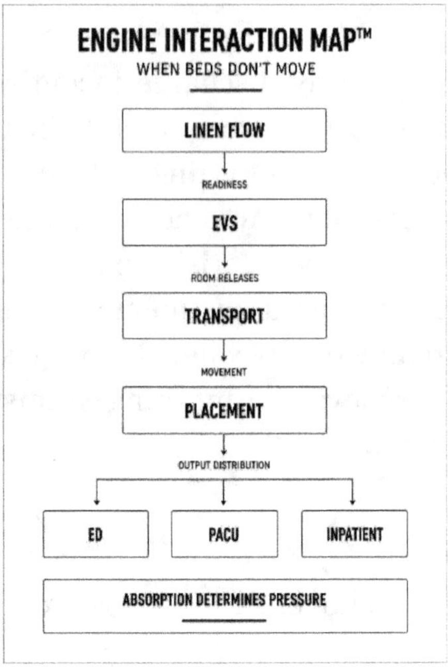

Figure 12: Engine Interaction Map

Next: Seeing the System as One

All seven engines have now been revealed. The next question is not where flow breaks. It is why hospitals tolerate drift long before they fix it, and how leaders learn to see the system clearly enough to intervene before the pressure announces itself.

PART THREE
Holding the System

Leadership, discipline, and the daily practice of flow

CHAPTER 10

Seeing the System as One

Why Flow Breaks Are Tolerated Long Before They Are Fixed

Hospitals do not fail suddenly. They drift.

Drift is tolerated far longer than leaders realize.

By the time breakdowns are visible, the system has already accepted weeks or months of misalignment as normal. Flow does not collapse from one miss. It collapses from a pattern leaders stopped seeing.

This chapter is about restoring sight.

Why Leaders Miss Flow Breaks

Most leaders are trained to see performance by department.

They review:

- staffing
- productivity
- length of stay
- throughput
- cost

Flow breaks rarely announce themselves as failures. They appear as:

- small delays
- reasonable workarounds

- justified exceptions
- localized explanations

Each one makes sense in isolation. Together, they create drift.

Leaders do not ignore flow. They are rarely taught how to see it.

Flow Is Not a Process, It Is a Condition

Processes describe steps. Flow describes whether movement is possible.

A hospital can have strong processes and broken flow.

Flow exists when:

- readiness appears on time
- movement stays evenly spaced
- pressure is released predictably
- absorption occurs without rebound

When any of these fail, flow degrades, even if departments appear to be performing well.

This is why flow problems persist. No single area owns the condition.

Drift Becomes Invisible When It Is Normalized

Drift begins as a minor miss:

- a late discharge
- a delayed room

- a held admit
- a stalled transfer

The system compensates. People stretch. Workarounds appear.

Soon, leaders hear:

- "That's just how mornings go."
- "ED always backs up around noon."
- "PACU is always tight after the first wave."

Drift has become expectation. Once normalized, drift no longer triggers concern. It becomes background noise.

The Cost of Drift Is Not Where You Look

And yet the cost is real. It just hides.

Drift rarely shows up cleanly on reports. It hides in:

- staff fatigue
- patient wait perception
- quiet OR inefficiency
- extended LOS
- throughput ceilings
- cultural resignation

Hospitals spend years chasing visible symptoms while drift quietly limits capacity.

Flow is usually lost long before revenue is.

How to Read the Hospital as a System

Seeing flow requires different questions.

Not:

- "Is the ED busy?"
- "Are beds full?"
- "Is PACU staffed?"

But:

- "Where did movement slow first today?"
- "Which engine absorbed pressure quietly?"
- "Which release window was missed?"
- "Where did pressure rebound upstream?"

These questions reveal physics, not performance.

Early Warning Signals Leaders Often Miss

Flow almost always warns before it fails.

Early signals include:

- compressed morning windows
- uneven admission spacing
- silent holds instead of escalation
- increased rework
- repeated temporary fixes

These are not operational annoyances. They are system alarms.

Leaders who learn to see them intervene earlier, with far less force.

Why Flow Cannot Be Fixed Locally

Departments optimize locally to survive pressure. That optimization is rational. It is also destabilizing.

When each engine protects itself:

- readiness slips
- motion batches
- balance breaks
- pressure rebounds

Local excellence does not guarantee system flow. Only alignment does.

Seeing the system does not replace operational management. It prevents drift from becoming invisible. The pace of the hospital is set by its alignment, not its effort, not the speed of effort. When leaders see that alignment clearly, flow improves with surprisingly little force.

The work of holding that alignment is what Leadership Discipline addresses directly.

What System Sight Reveals

Once a leader begins reading the hospital as a system rather than a collection of departments, several things become immediately visible that were invisible before.

The first is the gap between activity and movement. Most hospitals are full of task completion. The morning meeting happened. The discharge plans were documented. The assignments were posted. Yet the hospital is not moving. Tasks and movement are not the same thing, and leaders trained to manage tasks will miss the flow problem entirely.

The second is the timing of pressure. Pressure that appears to arrive suddenly in the ED at 10:00 a.m. has been building since 6:30 a.m. The visible problem and the causal problem are separated by hours. Leaders who read timing rather than outcomes can find the cause before it becomes the crisis.

The third is the location of real leverage. Flow almost never improves where leaders apply force. It improves one or two engines upstream from where pressure is visible. A leader who sees the system knows where to intervene. A leader who sees departments knows only where to escalate.

The Three Conversations That Change

When leaders shift to a system lens, three recurring conversations change in structure and in outcome.

The morning escalation call changes from a reporting exercise to a timing diagnosis. Instead of asking which department is behind, leaders ask which activation window was missed and what the downstream signal was. The question changes the answer. The answer changes the intervention.

The capacity meeting changes from a census review to a flow audit. Instead of counting beds, leaders read sequence. Which releases are clustering? Which engines are absorbing pressure they did not create? Where is absorption breaking down? These questions surface the real constraint faster than any dashboard.

The performance conversation changes from a personnel issue to a physics issue. When a leader understands that Transport is not slow, it is absorbing burst requests from misaligned upstream releases, the conversation becomes a coordination problem rather than a staffing problem. The solution changes accordingly.

How Hospitals Begin to Self-Correct

System sight does not require a new structure. It requires a new question. Hospitals that begin asking where movement slowed first rather than who is responsible begin to self-correct without leadership force.

This happens because the question surfaces the right information. When the right information surfaces at the right time, small corrections become possible before large failures are required. The hospital does not need more urgency. It needs better sight.

The shift from reactive to proactive is not a culture change. It is a question change. And it begins the moment a leader stops looking at outcomes and starts reading timing.

What Seeing the System Looks Like in Practice: A Composite Case

At a 380-bed regional health system, a CNO began attending the 7:00 a.m. transport dispatch window three days per week. She was not there to supervise. She was there to watch timing. Within two weeks she identified a pattern: the first cluster of Transport requests arrived within four minutes of each other on days when EVS had released rooms in geographic sequence rather than placement priority. On those days, ED holds by 9:00 a.m. were consistently higher.

She did not escalate EVS. She asked one question: what would the morning look like if the first three room releases matched the top three placement priorities? The EVS director tried it for a week. Mid-morning Transport clustering dropped on four of the five days. ED holds before 9:00 a.m. improved consistently in the following month.

> *No project was launched. No dashboard was built. A leader saw the system, asked one question, and made one small adjustment. Composite scenario representing patterns observed across multiple hospital assessments.*

The engines have been revealed. The system has been named.

What remains is the will to see it every morning before it breaks.

Hospitals do not fail because leaders stop caring.

They fail because leaders stop seeing.

The leader who reads timing rather than outcomes will always intervene earlier, with less force, and produce more durable results than the leader who waits for the escalation call. That capacity, to see the system before it announces itself, is what the next three chapters are about.

Next: Leadership Discipline

Seeing the system is the first act. Protecting it is the second. Chapter 11 shows what it takes to hold flow in practice, not through heroics, but through the quiet consistency that prevents drift from forming in the first place.

CHAPTER 11

Leadership Discipline

How Flow Is Actually Protected

Flow does not fail because leaders stop caring. It fails because discipline drifts.

Discipline is not enforcement. It is the quiet consistency that prevents timing from slipping in the first place.

Hospitals with stable flow do not have better intentions. They have better discipline.

Discipline Is Not Control

Many leaders equate discipline with control:

- rules
- audits
- escalation
- compliance

Control reacts after failure. Discipline prevents failure from forming.

Discipline protects timing and sequence, not people. It intervenes early, quietly, and predictably.

The more control leaders apply, the more workarounds appear. The more discipline they apply, the fewer exceptions are needed.

Where Discipline Actually Lives

Discipline does not live in meetings or reports. It lives in moments.

It shows up when leaders:

- protect activation windows
- interrupt normalization of delay
- refuse "just for today" exceptions
- correct sequence before speed
- intervene before escalation is required

These moments are small. Their impact is not.

Flow is lost in minutes, not months. Discipline protects those minutes.

Why Leaders Intervene Too Late

Most leaders intervene at outcomes:

- ED boarding
- OR delays
- PACU holds
- staffing shortages

By then, discipline has already failed upstream.

Early intervention feels unnecessary. Late intervention feels urgent.

Discipline chooses the unnecessary moments. Reaction inherits the urgent ones.

How Good Intentions Create Drift

Drift rarely begins with negligence. It begins with accommodation.

Common examples:

- allowing late discharges to slide
- approving uneven admissions
- tolerating small holds
- excusing missed windows
- protecting local convenience

Each decision feels reasonable. Together, they normalize misalignment.

Discipline is the refusal to let "reasonable" become routine.

Disciplined Leadership Is Boring, And Effective

Disciplined leaders:

- show up early to the same moments
- ask the same timing questions
- make the same small corrections
- protect rhythm without drama

This does not feel heroic. It feels repetitive.

That repetition is what holds flow.

Hospitals do not drift because leaders are absent. They drift because leaders stop being consistent.

What Discipline Is Not

Discipline is not:

- micromanagement
- constant oversight
- zero tolerance
- perfection

Discipline allows flexibility within boundaries. It protects the system without suffocating it.

Rigid leadership breaks flow. Undisciplined leadership dissolves it.

The Quiet Power of Early Correction

Early correction is invisible to most people. That invisibility is the point.

When leaders correct drift early:

- escalation is unnecessary
- staff stress decreases
- trust increases
- rhythm holds

The absence of crisis is the signal of discipline.

Flow does not require force. It requires consistency. When leaders apply discipline early and evenly, flow stabilizes with surprisingly little effort. When they don't, no amount of urgency can recover lost rhythm. Discipline is not what leaders do when things go wrong. It is what they protect so things don't.

What Discipline Looks Like at Each Engine

At Engine 0, discipline means verifying linen closet readiness before EVS activates, not after a miss is reported. It means checking stocking sequence on Sunday evening rather than calling a Monday morning meeting. The leader who rounds on a linen closet at 6:45 a.m. is not micromanaging. They are protecting the first engine.

At Engine 1, discipline means enforcing room release sequence by placement priority rather than allowing geographic convenience to govern the morning. It means correcting a sequence drift the moment it appears, not at the escalation call. The EVS supervisor who stops a team at 7:05 a.m. to redirect the first room is not slowing the morning. They are saving the afternoon.

At Engine 2, discipline means watching for request clustering before it becomes burst absorption. A transport coordinator who sees two requests arrive within three minutes of each other and flags the pattern to placement is practicing upstream discipline. Two requests is a warning. Four is a cascade.

At Engine 3, discipline means holding placement sequence when urgency from the ED pushes for the fastest available bed rather than the right one. The placement coordinator who declines to fill a unit already at bandwidth, even when the ED is pressuring, is not being unresponsive. They are preventing a rebound that will cost the ED three hours of holding by afternoon.

The Moment Most Leaders Miss

Leadership discipline fails most often not in a dramatic decision but in a quiet accommodation. Someone asks for a one-time exception. A window slips by a few minutes. An approval comes through slightly out of sequence. Each of these feels harmless.

But discipline is not a single decision. It is a pattern. The exception that felt harmless on Monday becomes the precedent that is assumed on Wednesday. By Friday it is the new standard. By the following month it is what people call normal.

This is why the moment discipline matters most is the moment when compliance feels unnecessary. When everything looks fine. When no alarm has fired. When teams are working and the day feels manageable. That is precisely the moment leaders must protect timing, because the cost of discipline is invisible and the cost of its absence is delayed.

How Discipline Erodes

Discipline does not collapse suddenly. It erodes through a predictable sequence that repeats across hospitals of every size.

First, a window slips without consequence. The day still ran. The outcome was acceptable. The miss gets filed away as an anomaly.

Second, the slip is accommodated rather than corrected. A workaround appears. People adapt. The system compensates. Leaders see the compensation and assume the system is resilient.

Third, the accommodation becomes routine. The workaround is now the process. No one remembers what the original standard was. Leaders begin managing the workaround rather than the root timing.

Fourth, pressure builds. The workaround reaches its limit. What was manageable becomes a crisis. Leaders escalate, add resources, and call for improvement. The improvement addresses the symptom. The window that started the sequence is never examined.

Discipline prevents the first step. Nothing else in this chain matters if the first slip is corrected immediately.

Leadership Discipline in Practice: A Composite Case

At a 290-bed community hospital, the house supervisor began a single habit: every morning at 7:10 a.m., she confirmed the first Transport move had occurred. Not by checking a dashboard. By calling the Transport coordinator directly.

For the first two weeks, the move had happened by 7:10 a.m. on eight of ten days. On the two days it had not, she asked one question: what changed this morning? Both times, the answer traced to a linen sequence issue from the night before.

She brought the pattern to the EVS director. They added a 6:45 a.m. closet confirmation to the evening supervisor checklist. Within three weeks, the first Transport move was occurring by 7:08 a.m. on nine of ten days. ED holds before 9:30 a.m. declined. PACU reported fewer morning holds. The OR ran its first two weeks of on-time afternoon completions in over a year.

The house supervisor did not launch a project. She asked one question, at the same time, every day. That consistency was discipline. Everything else followed from it.

> *Composite scenario representing patterns observed across multiple hospital assessments.*

Discipline holds flow in the moment. Resilient systems hold it over time. The next chapter shows how aligned systems detect drift early and correct it before leaders ever need to intervene.

Next: Drift Prevention

Discipline keeps the system aligned in the moment. Drift Prevention explains how to build systems that hold alignment over time, so that early correction becomes structural rather than heroic.

CHAPTER 12

Drift Prevention

Why Stable Systems Self-Correct While Others Don't

Drift is not a failure. It is a property of complex systems.

Every hospital drifts.

The difference between stable hospitals and struggling ones is not whether drift occurs, it is whether drift is corrected before it settles.

Drift prevention is not vigilance. It is design.

Drift Is Inevitable, Settling Is Not

No system holds perfect alignment indefinitely.

Timing slips. Sequencing fractures. Pressure accumulates.

In resilient systems, these shifts are corrected early. In fragile systems, they are tolerated.

Drift becomes dangerous only when it is allowed to settle into routine.

Why Drift Returns After Successful Fixes

Hospitals often fix flow, temporarily.

Metrics improve. Pressure eases. Leaders relax. Then drift returns.

This happens because most fixes address symptoms, not detection. They correct outcomes without strengthening early correction.

When attention fades, drift re-enters unnoticed.

Stability is not achieved. It is maintained.

Fragile Flow vs. Resilient Flow

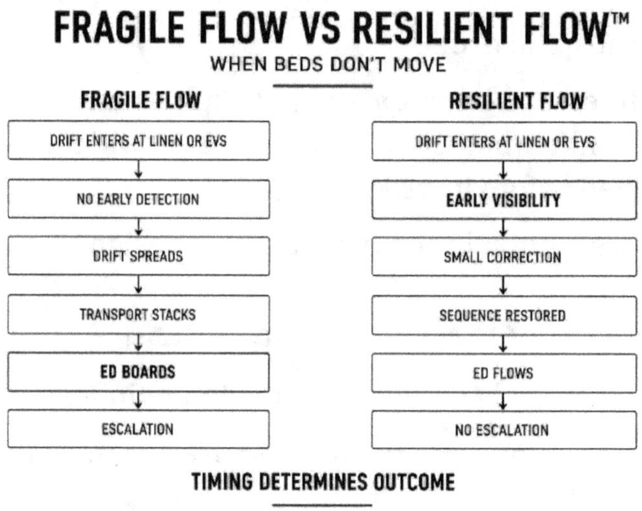

Figure 13: Fragile Flow vs. Resilient Flow

Fragile systems rely on people compensating. Resilient systems rely on rhythm holding.

In fragile systems:

- leaders intervene late
- escalation is frequent
- workarounds proliferate
- pressure feels constant

In resilient systems:

- correction happens early

- escalation is rare
- rhythm self-restores
- pressure dissipates quietly

Resilience is not busyness. It is predictability.

Early Correction Is the Core Mechanism

Early correction does not feel urgent. That is why it is often missed.

It looks like:

- adjusting sequence before queues form
- protecting a release window quietly
- spacing movement before compression appears
- addressing timing before outcomes shift

These corrections are small. Their impact is large.

Waiting for confirmation creates failure. Correction must occur before certainty.

Why Standardization Alone Fails

Early correction is the right mechanism. But early correction requires something standardization cannot provide: adaptive timing awareness.

Standardization freezes process. Drift moves through timing.

A hospital can be perfectly standardized and still misaligned.

When leaders rely only on standards:

- variation hides in timing
- sequence erodes silently
- pressure accumulates invisibly

Standards support flow. They do not preserve it.

Drift prevention requires adaptive awareness, not rigid enforcement.

Standardization vs. Timing: How a Compliant Process Still Fails

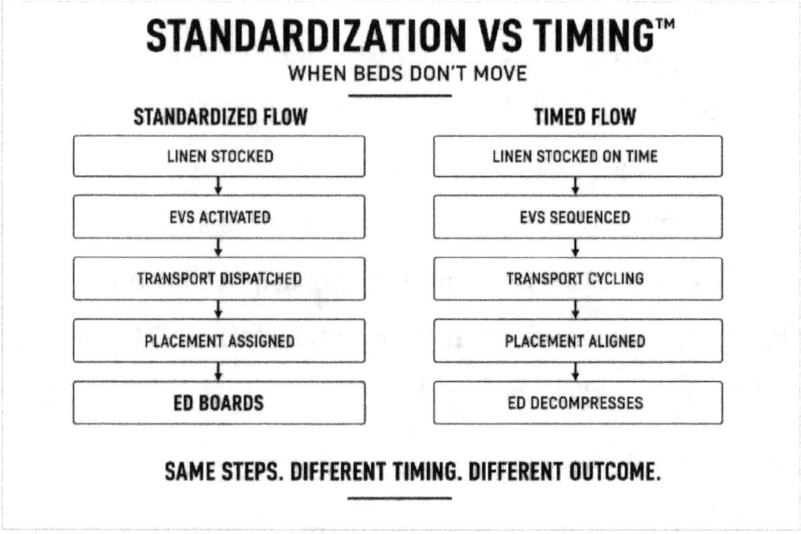

Figure 14: Standardization vs. Timing

Process Step

Standardized Process

Cycle Velocity Breakdown

Result

Linen stocking

Par levels met. Closets stocked by 6:30 a.m. Standard followed.

High-use items stocked in wrong sequence. First-room supplies are at the back of the closet.

EVS detours. Activation Window missed. Day starts behind.

EVS room assignment

Assignments made by geographic zone. Standard protocol followed.

Geographic zone does not match placement priority. High-demand rooms cleaned last.

Transport stacks. Placement loses rhythm. ED holds grow.

Transport dispatch

Requests dispatched as received. Response time standard met.

EVS released three rooms in one burst. Four requests arrived simultaneously. Cycle velocity collapsed.

Nursing receives admits in batches. Bandwidth saturates. Hold requested.

Placement sequencing

Bed assigned within 10 minutes of request. Placement protocol met.

Beds filled by availability, not unit bandwidth. One unit absorbing three consecutive admits.

Unit saturates. ED boarding extends. PACU unable to release.

Discharge planning

Discharge plans documented for all appropriate patients. Compliance rate above 90 percent.

All discharges executing between 1:00 and 3:00 p.m. Morning admission window receives no capacity relief.

Afternoon crisis. PACU holds. OR compression. ED boarding throughout the day.

> *In every row above, the standard was met. The process was followed. The day still failed. The variable in each case was not compliance. It was timing.*

Self-Correcting Systems

Self-correcting systems share common traits:

- early visibility across engines
- shared understanding of timing
- trust between functions
- predictable handoffs
- consistent escalation thresholds

These traits allow small corrections to occur without drama.

Flow stabilizes not because people work harder, but because the system notices drift early.

Why Leadership Matters, But Is Not Central

Leaders enable drift prevention. They do not execute it alone.

When leaders:

- protect early correction
- reinforce rhythm
- resist tolerance creep
- preserve system visibility

The organization corrects itself.

When leaders wait for problems to escalate, self-correction collapses.

Drift does not destroy systems. Settled drift does. Hospitals fail slowly, then suddenly. The difference between those outcomes is early correction. Resilient systems do not avoid drift. They prevent it from becoming normal.

Building Detection Into the System

Drift prevention does not require leaders to watch everything. It requires the system to surface the right signals at the right time so that small corrections remain possible.

Detection starts with agreement on what normal looks like. Most hospitals have not defined normal operationally. They have defined it culturally, which means normal is whatever happened yesterday. When yesterday included drift, normal includes drift. The baseline keeps shifting.

Operationally defined normal means specifying the timing thresholds that represent alignment. First Movement Time by 7:20 a.m. EVS first room entry by 7:05 a.m. Transport first move completed within 18 minutes of room release. Placement first admission confirmation within 12 minutes of bed assignment. These are not targets. They are drift detectors. When performance falls outside these thresholds, early correction is triggered without escalation.

The difference between a hospital that self-corrects and one that does not is whether these thresholds are visible and owned. Visible means leaders can see them without calling a meeting. Owned means a specific role is responsible for each window, not a committee, not a department, a person.

What Early Correction Requires

Early correction has three requirements that most hospitals do not yet have in place.

The first is threshold agreement. Leaders must know what Yellow looks like before it arrives. If the Yellow threshold for Transport is three simultaneous requests, the correction is to space the next release, not to add a transporter. But if no one has defined the threshold, no one recognizes Yellow. They wait for Red, and Red is already too late.

The second is response clarity. When a Yellow signal fires, what happens next must be agreed upon in advance. Ambiguous response creates delay. Delay turns Yellow to Red. A self-correcting system has a short, clear correction for each Yellow threshold. The correction is smaller than it would be at Red. That is the point.

The third is authority at the right level. Most hospitals require escalation to respond to drift. Escalation takes time. By the time approval arrives, the correction window has closed. Drift prevention requires the person closest to the signal to have authority to make the small correction without approval. This is not autonomy without accountability. It is designed delegation.

The Architecture of a Self-Correcting System

A self-correcting system has four structural properties that distinguish it from a system dependent on leadership heroics.

Shared visibility means that EVS, Transport, Placement, and Nursing can each see enough of the adjacent engine to know when sequencing is drifting. They do not need a unified command center. They need enough adjacent visibility to catch their own intake before it compresses the next engine.

Predictable handoffs mean that each engine knows what it will receive from the engine before it, in what sequence, and approximately when. Predictability reduces the need for coordination by eliminating the uncertainty that generates unnecessary communication.

Threshold-triggered correction means that when a defined signal appears, a defined response follows. No meeting required. No approval required. The response is agreed in advance and proportional to the signal. This is what allows small corrections to stay small.

Leadership reinforcement means that leaders protect the system rather than substitute for it. When a hospital relies on a strong leader to hold flow, flow fails when that leader is absent. When a hospital builds self-correction into the architecture, flow holds whether or not the best leader is in the building that day.

Drift Prevention in Practice: A Composite Case

A 475-bed regional medical center had invested two years in throughput improvement with mixed results. Metrics would improve for six to eight weeks after each initiative, then drift back toward baseline. Leaders recognized the pattern but could not sustain the gains.

An operational review identified the root issue: the hospital had excellent fix capacity but no detection architecture. When drift returned, no one saw it until escalation was required. By then, the correction required was large, expensive, and disruptive.

Over ninety days, the hospital built three operational thresholds with defined Yellow signals and pre-approved responses: a 7:20 a.m. FMT target with a named coordinator; a Transport clustering threshold of three simultaneous requests triggering a staggered release request to EVS; and a placement bandwidth check every 45 minutes during the morning window.

In the first month after implementation, one escalation call occurred in the morning window, down from an average of four per week. In the second month, drift that would previously have required a two-hour intervention was corrected in under twenty minutes on three separate occasions. The corrections required no additional staff and no new technology. They required early visibility and pre-agreed responses.

> *Composite scenario representing patterns observed across multiple hospital assessments.*

Drift prevention keeps systems aligned over time. But alignment only lasts when leaders choose to protect it, daily. The final chapter is about that choice.

Next: Flow as a Posture

Detection architecture sustains flow over weeks and months. The final chapter is about something more fundamental: the leadership identity that makes sustained flow possible at all. Flow is not a project. It is a posture. And posture is a choice.

CHAPTER 13

Flow as a Posture

Why Flow Is Not a Project

Hospitals do not lose flow because they stop trying. They lose flow because posture does not change.

Projects end. Posture endures.

Flow is not something a hospital installs, launches, or completes. It is how the organization chooses to operate, every day.

Why Flow Projects Always Fail

Hospitals are excellent at projects. They create:

- task forces
- dashboards
- initiatives
- timelines
- milestones

For a while, flow improves. Then attention shifts. Ownership diffuses. Urgency fades. Flow degrades again.

This happens because projects target outcomes. Flow depends on alignment.

When the project ends, posture reverts.

Flow Is Held in Daily Decisions

Flow does not live in strategy decks. It lives in moments leaders barely notice.

It is held when leaders:

- protect timing instead of convenience
- preserve sequence instead of speed
- intervene early instead of loudly
- refuse normalization of drift
- choose alignment over accommodation

These decisions are not dramatic. They are repetitive.

That repetition is posture.

Why Culture Is the Wrong Target

Hospitals often try to "fix culture" to sustain flow. Culture follows posture. It does not create it.

When leaders hold alignment consistently:

- behavior stabilizes
- expectations clarify
- trust increases
- culture shifts

When leaders tolerate drift:

- workarounds multiply
- frustration grows
- cynicism spreads

Culture is the shadow of leadership posture.

What Strong Systems Refuse to Tolerate

Hospitals that sustain flow are not stricter. They are clearer.

They quietly refuse:

- chronic lateness
- normalized holds
- silent batching
- workaround pride
- drift language

Not through punishment. Through consistency.

What leaders tolerate becomes policy, whether written or not.

Why the Best Systems Look Uneventful

Stable flow does not look impressive. There are:

- fewer escalations
- fewer heroics
- fewer emergencies
- fewer urgent meetings

Days feel ordinary. Movement feels smooth. Pressure dissipates quietly.

This often worries leaders accustomed to constant urgency.

Uneventful is not complacent. Uneventful is aligned.

Flow as a Leadership Identity

At some point, flow stops being an initiative and becomes identity.

Leaders stop asking:

"How do we fix flow?"

And start asking:

"What posture are we holding today?"

That question changes decisions immediately.

Flow holds not because leaders remember a framework, but because alignment becomes instinctive.

Where to Begin

Every hospital described in this book had leaders who wanted things to be better. Most were working hard. The systems were failing anyway, not because of effort, but because the right things weren't being protected.

If you've read this far, you already see the system differently. The question now is where to apply that seeing first.

The answer is almost always the same: start with the morning.

In your first thirty days, make three observations and three decisions:

1. Observe First Movement Time™.

Begin tracking the timestamp of your hospital's first confirmed patient move each morning. Do not average it yet. Just see it. What time does movement actually begin? Who owns that window? What happens on days it slips past 7:45 a.m.? This is an observation, not a project. The number will tell you more about your system's health than most dashboards you currently review.

2. Name what you observe in your building.

Walk your morning. Not to round on people, to see timing. Identify the stretch where your hospital is active but not moving. Listen for the language: "that's just how mornings go," "we're waiting on...," "that's normal for us." Each phrase is a marker of normalized drift. This is an observation. Name it. You cannot make a decision about something you have not yet seen. You cannot close a Stagnation Gap™ you have not named.

3. Make one decision and hold it.

You do not need to fix all seven engines at once. Choose the one engine where early misalignment causes the most downstream pain in your hospital, often Linen, EVS, or Placement. Define its Activation Window™. Assign ownership. Begin protecting it. This is a decision, not an initiative. One protected window, held consistently, will reveal more about your system than months of dashboards.

These are not projects. They are observations and decisions.

The goal of the first thirty days is not transformation. It is not a project. It is clarity.

Observe the timing. Name what you see. Decide what to protect.

From there, the system begins to open.

And it begins the moment a leader decides to see the system for what it is.

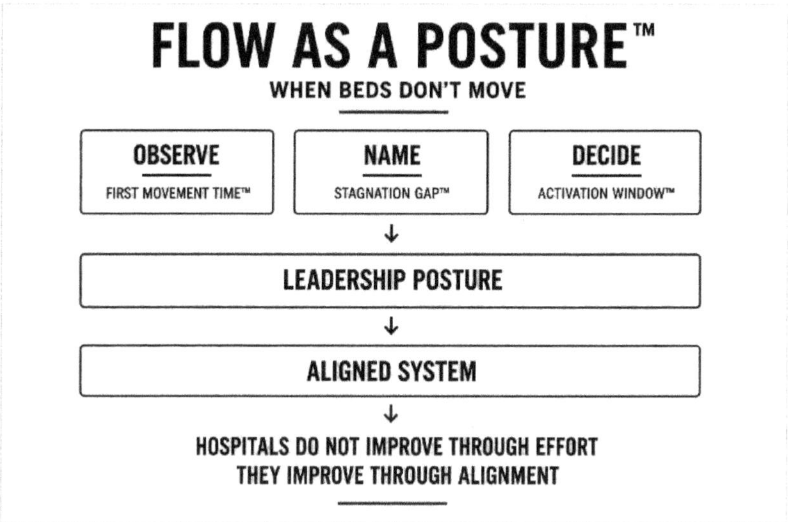

Figure 15: Flow as a Posture

Hospitals do not move better because they try harder.

They move better because leaders protect alignment, every day.

Flow is not an initiative. It is not a program. It is not a project.

Flow is a posture.

A posture does not need a launch date.

It does not need a committee, a kickoff meeting, or a slide deck.

It needs a leader who decides, today, to see the system for what it is.

To protect the timing.

To hold the window.

To let the morning prove what the system is capable of.

The beds will move.

Glossary of Proprietary Terms

The terms defined in this glossary are proprietary conceptual systems developed by Donald Sipp Jr. They describe original methodologies for diagnosing, explaining, and stabilizing hospital patient flow. Each term carries a trademark designation (™) and may not be reproduced, redistributed, or applied in commercial contexts without written permission.

Activation Miss™

The failure of a department or engine to begin its first cycle within its designated Activation Window™. An Activation Miss does not always register as an incident. It registers as a delay that the next engine must absorb without explanation.

> *Note: Distinguished from staffing shortage or communication failure. An Activation Miss is a timing failure, not a people failure.*

Activation Window™

The specific time window within which a department or engine must begin its first cycle to sustain downstream flow. Activation Windows are not shift start times. They are operational thresholds. When a department enters its Activation Window on time, it passes momentum forward. When it misses, it passes pressure forward.

> *Note: Every engine in the Flow Physics™ framework has a distinct Activation Window. Protecting Activation Windows is the primary mechanism of flow leadership.*

Cycle Loss™

The cumulative erosion of operational throughput caused by small timing deviations that compound across cycles. Cycle Loss is not a single failure. It is the quiet math of repeated small slips accumulating into a measurable reduction in daily capacity. As Cycle Loss accumulates, Cycle Velocity™ drops: the engine completes fewer cycles per hour, and downstream engines wait longer between each one.

Cycle Velocity™

The rate at which an engine completes its operational cycles within a given time window. Cycle Velocity is the speed of the system, not the speed of any individual worker. When Cycle Velocity drops, the engine produces fewer outputs per hour, and downstream engines wait.

Drift™

The gradual, often undetected departure of an operational system from its designed timing and sequencing. Drift is not a breakdown. It is the period before a breakdown, when conditions are worsening but no alarm has fired. Drift that is normalized becomes invisible. Invisible drift becomes the new standard.

> *Note: Drift is the central diagnostic concept of Flow Physics™. The framework exists to detect and interrupt Drift before it compounds into system pressure.*

Engine Misalignment™

The condition in which two or more engines are operating on incompatible timing or sequencing assumptions, causing friction at handoff points. Engine Misalignment is not always caused by error. It is often caused by each engine optimizing locally without visibility into the whole system.

Engine 0™ through Engine 6™

The seven operational engines that together constitute hospital flow, numbered in order of upstream to downstream position. Engine 0 (Linen Flow™) is the foundation. Engine 6 (Inpatient Units) is the final absorber. All seven engines must operate in sequence and rhythm for the hospital to move predictably.

> *Note: The seven engines: Engine 0 (Linen Flow), Engine 1 (EVS), Engine 2 (Transport Flow), Engine 3 (Placement Flow), Engine 4 (ED Flow), Engine 5 (PACU Flow), Engine 6 (Inpatient Unit Flow).*

First Movement Time™ (FMT™)

The timestamp of the first confirmed patient movement of the operational day. First Movement Time is the single most predictive operational metric in hospital flow. Days when FMT is early and protected tend toward alignment. Days when FMT is late or unowned tend toward escalation.

> *Note: FMT is not an average. It is a single daily timestamp. The discipline of tracking it is the discipline of owning the morning.*

First Room Rule™

The operational principle that the first room EVS enters sets the pace for every room that follows, and therefore for every downstream engine. The First Room Rule describes the hinge point where invisible upstream conditions become visible operational outcomes. A strong first room passes momentum forward. A compromised first room passes pressure forward.

Flow as a Posture™

The leadership identity described in Flow as a Posture: the understanding that flow is not a project, program, or initiative, but a daily discipline of observation, naming, and protection. A leader with a flow posture does not wait for Red signals. They make small decisions early to prevent Red from arriving.

Flow Operating System™

The complete operational system that governs patient movement inside a hospital. The Flow Operating System™ encompasses all seven engines, the laws of Flow Physics™, the Activation Windows™ that connect them, and the governance disciplines required to hold them in alignment. The Flow Operating System is not a program a hospital installs. It is a description of forces already operating inside every hospital every day. The question is whether those forces are aligned or quietly compounding against the organization.

Flow Physics™

The proprietary operational framework developed by Donald Sipp Jr. for diagnosing, explaining, and stabilizing hospital patient flow. Flow Physics holds that hospitals are governed by discoverable operational laws, not random complexity, and that drift, pressure, and collapse are predictable when the right signals are observed.

> *Note: Flow Physics is not a methodology for improving individual departments. It is a systems lens for reading the hospital as a single, interdependent operational organism.*

Linen Flow™

Engine 0 in the Flow Physics™ framework. Linen Flow encompasses all the processes, timing dependencies, and sequencing decisions that determine whether linen is available, correctly stocked, and properly sequenced before EVS activates. Linen Flow is invisible to most hospital leaders. Its failures are visible to everyone.

Linen Flow Cycle™

The complete eight-step operational cycle that sustains reliable linen delivery: Forecast, Build, Sequence, Deliver, Stock, Verify, Monitor, and Replenish. Hospitals operating on an abbreviated three-step cycle (Deliver, Stock, Replenish) lack the visibility and verification steps that catch drift before it reaches EVS.

Linen Flow Demand Variance™

The unit-specific variation in linen consumption patterns that makes uniform stocking a systematic generator of drift. Each unit type (ICU, Med/Surg, Surgical, ED, Labor and Delivery) has a distinct demand curve. Stocking every unit identically guarantees mismatch and drift on high-demand units.

Linen Geography Problem™

The operational constraint created by closet placement, layout, and distance that forces EVS technicians to travel farther than necessary to retrieve and stock linen. Geography that was not engineered intentionally for workflow creates drift even when par levels are correct and timing is protected.

Load Multiplication™

The compounding effect by which a small upstream delay generates a disproportionately larger downstream workload. Load Multiplication explains why a five-minute Linen miss can produce a two-hour ED boarding crisis. The math is not linear. Early pressure amplifies as it travels downstream.

Patient Flow Paradox™

The condition in which a hospital has physically available beds but cannot move patients into them because the operational engines required to activate those beds are misaligned. The Patient Flow Paradox explains why capacity on paper does not equal capacity in practice. Beds only matter when they can be activated at the moment a patient needs them. When timing, sequencing, or readiness fails, the hospital functions as if it is full, even when it is not.

Pressure Signal™

The operational indicator that an engine is approaching or has exceeded its capacity to absorb upstream drift without generating downstream impact. Pressure Signals exist at both the Yellow and Red thresholds. The Yellow Pressure Signal is the correctable moment. The Red Pressure Signal is the management moment.

Readiness Engine™

A descriptor for Engine 0 (Linen Flow™) reflecting its foundational role in the operational system. The Readiness Engine does not move patients. It creates the conditions under which all patient-moving engines can activate. Without readiness, movement cannot begin on time.

Seven-Day Rhythm™

The weekly operational pattern that governs linen demand, EVS staffing, and system pressure across different days of the week. Sunday-to-Monday transitions are the highest-risk period in the Seven-Day Rhythm. Weekend Drift™ that goes uncorrected by Sunday evening compounds into Monday morning pressure.

Stagnation Gap™

The period between shift start and first confirmed patient movement during which the hospital is active but not moving. The Stagnation Gap is characterized by task completion without flow output. It is the window where effort accumulates without advancing the system. Closing the Stagnation Gap requires sequencing work around movement triggers, not activity milestones.

> *Note: The Stagnation Gap is not a scheduling problem. It is an architecture problem. The same staff, same shift, same census can produce a 45-minute Gap or a two-hour Gap depending on what the morning is designed to protect.*

Support Services Chain™

The interdependent operational sequence of EVS, Transport, and Placement that together convert room readiness into patient movement. The Support Services Chain functions as a single operational unit. When any link in the chain operates on incompatible timing, the chain compresses and the ED absorbs the consequences.

Transport–Linen Lag Effect™

The downstream delay in Transport cycle velocity caused by upstream Linen Flow drift. When Linen Flow misses its Activation Window, EVS misses its Activation Window. When EVS misses, room releases are delayed. When room releases are delayed, Transport absorbs stacked requests rather than evenly spaced ones. The lag is not created by Transport. It is inherited by Transport.

Weekend Drift™

The operational degradation that accumulates across Saturday and Sunday due to reduced staffing patterns, altered routines, and lower correction frequency. Weekend Drift does not announce itself. It arrives Monday morning as a system that is already behind before the first patient moves.

Trademark Notice

Unauthorized reproduction, rebranding, training use, or commercial application of these frameworks without written permission from Donald Sipp Jr. is prohibited.

About the Author

Donald Sipp Jr.

MBA, RESE, CHESP, CHTI-2, CMIP, PMP

Capacity is rarely the true constraint in a hospital. Execution is. Donald Sipp Jr. has spent more than two decades inside hospitals proving it.

Donald is a healthcare operations consultant, educator, and thought leader specializing in non-clinical hospital operations: patient throughput, Environmental Services (EVS), patient transport, and linen management. He has led operational assessments and system-level transformations across hospitals and health systems nationwide, helping organizations reduce avoidable delays, strengthen bed turnaround reliability, and optimize labor utilization across the support services that keep patient flow moving.

He currently serves as a Senior Director with Ruck-Shockey Associates, Inc. and is the founder of Impact Training Company, where he develops practical training programs focused on leadership, accountability, and operational execution. He is the owner and credentialing authority of the Certified Healthcare Transporter (CHT) program, delivered in partnership with the National Association of Healthcare Transport Management (NAHTM), helping standardize transport practice and elevate transport teams as essential drivers of patient flow.

Across these engagements, he is known for rapidly diagnosing where work breaks down between departments and building simple, sustainable management systems that improve handoffs, restore daily operating discipline, and translate frontline effort into measurable throughput gains.

His expertise spans EVS, transport, and linen operations, with a consistent focus: integrating support functions into a cohesive operating system that sustains clinical care without friction or delay. He has helped organizations redesign linen distribution models, reduce loss, and better align supply with real-time patient demand across unit types with widely different consumption patterns.

Donald is a frequent national speaker who has delivered presentations on staffing optimization, patient throughput, and workforce performance at leading industry conferences. His insights have been featured in Infection Control Today and other healthcare operations publications. He also serves as an adjunct professor, bringing operational field experience into the classroom to prepare the next generation of healthcare and business leaders.

He wrote this book because the same pattern appears in every hospital he has assessed: leaders work hard, yet performance stalls because the system cannot execute at the right time, in the right sequence, with clear accountability. The constraint is rarely capacity. It is execution. This book gives hospital executives and operations leaders a practical framework for seeing what is actually happening, and acting on it.

Work With Donald Sipp Jr.

Healthcare operations consulting, keynote speaking, and leadership development.

Most hospitals are losing recoverable capacity every day without realizing it. The framework to find it already exists in this book. The work to apply it begins with a single conversation.

Donald Sipp Jr. works directly with hospital systems, health networks, and industry organizations to diagnose flow constraints, build operational architecture, and develop the leadership capacity to sustain it. If this book gave language to a problem that has resisted every previous fix, that problem is solvable. Here is where to start.

Operational Consulting

Most organizations begin with a Flow Physics™ Assessment.

This is a structured 2 to 3 day onsite review that maps your hospital's operational engines against the Flow Physics™ framework. The assessment produces a clear picture of where drift is forming, which Activation Windows™ are being missed, and where the highest-leverage corrections exist.

A Flow Physics™ Assessment includes:

- Engine alignment scoring across all eight operational engines, weighted by the impact of each criterion on downstream flow
- First Movement Time™ baseline. The single most predictive operational metric. Measured and sequenced against daily activation targets
- Stagnation Gap™ diagnostic. The window between shift start and first confirmed patient movement, revealing where the morning loses its rhythm before anyone notices
- Cycle Loss™ calculation. Recurring delays converted into bed-days lost, equivalent beds removed, and annual financial opportunity
- Constraint prioritization. Constraints ranked by impact and upstream position, so upstream causes are addressed before downstream symptoms
- 30-day sequenced action plan. Organized in three waves: stabilize the gate, open the converters, tune coordination and outputs
- Executive Brief. A single-page summary of the FPI score, top constraints, financial opportunity, and first actions, ready for leadership review

Engagements begin with the assessment and move into sequencing correction. Organizations building longer-term resilience follow with drift prevention architecture and leadership development.

Consulting engagements are available through Ruck-Shockey Associates, Inc., one of the nation's leading healthcare operations consulting and interim management firms.

Keynote and Conference Speaking

Donald is a national speaker who brings the frameworks in this book to live audiences. His presentations are built for hospital leaders, operations teams, and industry conferences where the audience needs more than inspiration. They need a system they can act on the following morning.

Speaking topics include:

- When Beds Don't Move: The Flow Physics™ of Hospital Operations
- The Hidden Engine: How Linen Flow Determines the Hospital Day
- First Movement Time: The Metric That Predicts Everything Else
- Drift Before Pressure: How to Lead Upstream
- From EVS to the ED: How the Support Services Chain™ Drives Flow
- Flow as a Posture: Leadership Identity in High-Performance Systems

Training and Credentialing

Through Impact Training Company and in partnership with the National Association of Healthcare Transport Management (NAHTM), Donald develops and delivers practical training programs for EVS, transport, and operations leaders at every level.

Programs include:

- Certified Healthcare Transporter Instructor (CHTI) credentialing program
- Linen Flow™ operations and sequencing workshops
- Flow Physics™ leadership development for department directors
- Operational accountability and execution training for frontline supervisors

The Next Step

If you recognized your hospital in these pages, the gap between where you are and where you could be is not a staffing problem or a culture problem. It is an architecture problem. Architecture can be corrected.

The fastest path forward is a conversation about what you're seeing and whether a Flow Physics™ Assessment makes sense for your organization.

Consulting: Ruck-Shockey Associates, Inc. |www.RuckShockey.com

Training: ImpactTrainingCompany.com

Email: Info@ImpactTrainingCompany.com

Credentialing: CHT Program | in partnership with NAHTM

The beds will move!

REFERENCES

FINANCIAL IMPACT OF EMERGENCY DEPARTMENT BOARDING

1. Canellas MM, Johnson MJ, Espinoza JL, Olufemi DO, Reznek MA. "Measurement of Cost of Boarding in the Emergency Department Using Time-Driven Activity-Based Costing." Annals of Emergency Medicine. Published online May 24, 2024. doi:10.1016/j.annemergmed.2024.04.012

2. Falvo T, Grove L, Stachura R, Vega D, Stachura M, Mackay D, Krishna A. "The Opportunity Loss of Boarding Admitted Patients in the Emergency Department." Academic Emergency Medicine. 2007;14(4):332-337. doi:10.1197/j.aem.2006.11.011

3. Beniuk K, Boyle AA, Rajagopalan S. "Emergency Department Crowding: Prioritising Quantified Crowding Measures to Evaluate and Respond to Crowding." Emergency Medicine Journal. 2012;29(6):477-481.

4. American College of Emergency Physicians. "Boarding Patients in Emergency Departments Nearly Doubles Daily Cost of Care, Study Finds." Press release, October 21, 2024. emergencyphysicians.org

FINANCIAL MODELING: BOARDING AND REVENUE RECOVERY

5. Pines JM, Batt RJ, Hilton JA, Terwiesch C. "The Financial Consequences of Lost Demand and Reducing Boarding in Hospital Emergency Departments." Annals of Emergency Medicine. 2011;58(4):331-340. doi:10.1016/j.annemergmed.2011.03.004

6. Bayley MD, Schwartz JS, Shofer FS, et al. "The Financial Burden of Emergency Department Congestion and Hospital Crowding for Chest Pain Patients Awaiting Admission." Annals of Emergency Medicine. 2005;45(2):110-117.

PACU BOARDING: COST AND LENGTH OF STAY IMPACT

7. Nelson DF, Palomino C, Torjman MC, Ooi G, Green MS. "Length of Stay and Cost of Care Differences Between Postoperative Patients Who Board in PACU and Those That Proceed Directly to Inpatient Bed." Perioperative Care and Operating Room Management. 2024;37:100434. doi:10.1016/j.pcorm.2024.100434

8. Pappada SM, Papadimos TJ, Khuder S, et al. "Contributing Factors to Operating Room Delays Identified from an Electronic Health Record: A Retrospective Study." Anesthesiology Research and Practice. 2022;2022:8635454. doi:10.1155/2022/8635454

PATIENT FLOW AND HOSPITAL OPERATIONAL RESEARCH

9. Institute of Medicine (US) Committee on the Future of Emergency Care in the United States Health System. Hospital-Based Emergency Care: At the Breaking Point. Washington, DC: National Academies Press; 2007.

10. Kelen GD, Wolfe R, D'Onofrio G, et al. "Emergency Department Crowding: The Canary in the Health Care System." NEJM Catalyst Innovations in Care Delivery. 2021;2(2). doi:10.1056/CAT.20.0217

11. American Hospital Association. "Patients and Providers Faced with Increasing Delays in Timely Discharges." Issue Brief. December 2022. aha.org

12. Agency for Healthcare Research and Quality. "AHRQ Summit to Address Emergency Department Boarding: Technical Report." December 2024. ahrq.gov

DISCHARGE TIMING AND CAPACITY MANAGEMENT

13. Artenstein AW, Rathlev NK, Neal D, et al. "Decreasing Emergency Department Walkout Rate and Boarding Hours by Improving Inpatient Length of Stay." Western Journal of Emergency Medicine. 2017;18(6):982-992. doi:10.5811/westjem.2017.7.34663

14. Strata Decision Technology. "Average Length-of-Stay Analysis: 2019 to 2022 Comparison." Cited in: American Hospital Association Issue Brief on Delayed Discharges, December 2022.

OPERATIONAL PERFORMANCE: TRANSPORT AND COMMAND CENTER DATA

15. Wright K, Wilkins H. "Driving Operational Excellence Through Command Center Performance Metrics and Analytics." Presented at: National Association of Healthcare Transport Managers Annual Conference; May 2024.

16. Cummins S, Daly N. "Tackling Barriers that Impact Turnaround Time for ED Admissions." Presented at: National Association of Healthcare Transport Managers Annual Conference; May 22, 2024.

> *The operational observations, case scenarios, and proprietary frameworks in this book are based on the author's direct field experience across more than two decades of hospital assessments. They do not constitute peer-reviewed research. The published sources listed above are cited to establish that independent research corroborates the financial and operational consequences described throughout the text.*

www.ingramcontent.com/pod-product-compliance
Lightning Source LLC
LaVergne TN
LVHW022216200926
848481LV00006B/1988

* 9 7 9 8 9 9 6 0 3 1 3 0 6 *